I0410503

Comparative Economics Islam's Panacea to maladies of Capitalism

Ibn Caesar

مكتبة اسلامية   MaktabaIslamia

MaktabaIslamia Publications

www.maktabaislamia.com
info@maktabaislamia.com
www.facebook.com/everythingislamic
www.twitter.com/maktabaislamia

Edition III: 1437 AH | 2016

The opinions within this book do not represent the views or beliefs of any organisation. All ideas that do not belong to the author have been cited accordingly.

For references to in-text citations please consult the bibliography.

For graphical explanations to economic theory, please consult the appendix when instructed.

Qur'anic Ayat and Ahadith have been translated and *italicised*. Typographic ligatures and their corresponding definitions:

ﷺ - صلى الله عليه وسلم (Peace be upon him)

ﷻ - جل جلاله (May his glory by glorified)

Preface: Since the caliphate's demise, Muslims have remained upon a path of ideological decline. From the depths of poverty to the brutality of war, we have passively endured the pain and suffering brought upon us for many years. Unable to realise the great significance of thought in resolving our metacognitive anaemia, economic recovery became a mere figment of our imagination and the caliphate, a glorious but obsolete history.

However, after decades in darkness Muslims have become increasingly agitated by the depravity that pervades them. What once started with dissent has now developed into a prodigious revolution across the Muslim world, characterised primarily by an overwhelming Islamic sentiment. At present, the caliphate is no longer perceived as a distant past but a near future, whose return has been made clear by Allah (ﷻ) in Surah An-Nur (55):

"Allah has promised, to those among you who believe and do righteous deeds, that He will, of a surety, grant them in the land, inheritance (of power), as He granted it to those before them; that He will establish in authority their religion, the one which He has chosen for them; and that He will change (their state), after the fear in which they (lived), to one of security and peace: They will worship Me (alone) and not associate aught with Me. If any do reject faith after this, they are rebellious and wicked."

Islam's imminent arrival has necessitated a vital discourse, in which its ability to purge the Muslim world of its economic woes must be explicated. This book seeks to do just that by briefly expanding upon the Islamic economic system through contemporary economic theory; introducing the subject of economics and the political economy, whilst highlighting key issues ingrained within the capitalist laissez-faire system.

Above all, it attempts to present Islam as a panacea to the maladies of capitalism by way of comparative analysis with the intent to extirpate (through revival) the ideological impotence that has plagued and obstructed our minds. In doing so, it will enable the reader to discern which ideology is more capable at solving key economic problems faced in our current reality.

TABLE OF CONTENTS

I. PROLOGUE: THE CURRENT PARADIGM

"The decadent international but individualistic capitalism in the hands of which we found ourselves after the war is not a success. It is not intelligent. It is not beautiful. It is not just. It is not virtuous. And it doesn't deliver the goods." - John Keynes[1]

In its youth, capitalism paved the way towards a new era of economic advancement and progression. From the industrial to the technological revolution, economists consistently praised the free market for its ability to achieve what was then putatively inconceivable. In the eyes of many, this prosperity was indicative of systemic success, but as time elapsed, capitalism abraded, and so too did the ostensible euphoria surrounding it. In fact, since its very inception capitalism has instigated many economic crises, invariably damaging its own ideological reputation, and in 2007-08 we witnessed the culmination of such decline in what many have hastened to label as 'the greatest calamity since the Great Depression'.

Post financial crisis, many attempts were made to elucidate capitalism's endogenous instability, but to no avail. Some economists focused entirely on institutional failure, others criticised the use of monetary and or fiscal policy, whilst many blamed human frailty and error, pushing liability from the economic system to those who managed it.[2] Within this ambitious investigation, one point became apparent; it is that capitalism has now matured (albeit not completely), in that its volatility has rapidly deteriorated and its cells have grown uncontrollably, giving birth to an aggressive cancer.

At present, the global economy currently suffers from a number of virulent macroeconomic problems such as severe resource misallocation, growing capital inequality, anaemic aggregate demand, irresponsible banking sectors, volatile financial markets, extortionate levels of private/public debt, large budget deficits, deteriorating balance of payments, rising levels of unemployment, poor monetary/fiscal policy, et cetera.

---

[1] Keynes, 1933
[2] Greenspan, 2013

It is quite clear that the limited success capitalism once enjoyed was merely an unsubstantiated boom, which misled many economists into believing that it was the ultimate salvation for mankind. Indeed, one needn't be an economist to prognosticate the free market's demise, nor a political scientist to fathom the fate of this ideology, rather the apotheosis of capitalism is intelligible, certainly based upon the aforementioned paradigm.

"It is impossible for capitalism to survive, primarily because the system of capitalism needs some blood to suck. Capitalism used to be like an eagle, but now it is more like a vulture. It used to be strong enough to go and suck anybody's blood whether they were strong or not. But now it has become more cowardly, like the vulture, and it can only suck the blood of the helpless. As the nations of the world free themselves, capitalism has less victims, less to suck, and it becomes weaker and weaker. It's only a matter of time in my opinion before it will collapse completely." - Malcolm X[3]

Amid this ideological atrophy, we find that the focal point of contemporary economics revolves around either the economic agent or economic policy. Such binary cognition has constraint man to the superficial and blinded him from the truth, which is that defects within both agent and policy are but the rotten fruits of a tree whose seed is congenitally corrupted. That is to analogically say; these issues are not the source of error, rather a product of it. Thus the true problem lies with the capitalist ideology, from which both variables originate.

It is therefore incumbent that we put an end to this economic recidivism by turning to an alternative ideology that resolves the basic human problems man is subject to. Let it be clear and well understood, the fundamental error of capitalism is its misjudgment of humans and their nature; it is the deep love for wealth within the hands of the few as opposed to the many, the imperative for growth at the expense of distribution, the amalgamation of the productive science with the distributive system, the extreme liberalisation of the market, et cetera.

Finally, it must be noted that the postulation of contemporary academics to ascertain the immutable has made the subject of economics eminently vapid. In chasing scientific objectivity, scholars have caged their minds from the rational truth. Such narrow thinking is rooted deep within the scientific method, which, post Enlightenment, became the modus operandi for success. It seems that social scientists have trapped themselves within the confines of this style of thought, due to either a firm conviction (in belief) or a growing fear (to dissent).

As for the former, a great number of sincere economists have been enticed by the strong empirical results of science and its method. They have internalised this style of thought and made it their own. To them we must say: the overwhelming success of the Enlightenment and what followed it thereafter, such as the Industrial Revolution, must not mask the inconsistencies in applying science to all of life's affairs. It cannot reach all conclusions, nor can it derive all truths, hence it must be used appropriately and restricted by its own limitations.

As for the latter, an equal number of insincere economists are well aware that such thinking is flawed but are fearful to contend the status quo. In this cognitive fear I sense cowardice, which is an odious trait, unbefitting the scholar. To them we must say: the pressure to conform must not supersede ones duty to make known what is true. There is no honour in defending falsehood, whilst there is great respect for those who promote the antithesis, which must be a duty upon the enlightened.

This book shall therefore pursue the raw truth, not seen through the prism of historical success, nor obscured by the blindfold of contemporary academic sensitivities. It will contest the current paradigm by explicating the Islamic economic system upon a rational basis, with the use of mathematics and science only where necessary and applicable. In doing so, this book shall then conclude that the most rational outcome for mankind is not for us to remain passive in our decline but to adopt the Islamic ideology as the only means to eradicate the pervasive problems of capitalism, that we are all a current witness to.

II. ECONOMIC IDEOLOGY

Synopsis: Rudimentary flaws in the ideology will inevitably cause greater problems within the macroeconomy. Islam is the only effective alternative to the inherent defects of capitalism.

At the centre of this comparative study, economists have tried relentlessly to render the Islamic economic system a mere extension of capitalism. However, all attempts hitherto have been utterly futile and are based primarily on selective comparisons between the characteristics of these ideologies, as opposed to their fundamental principles. Such an absurd endeavour (to link both systems upon superficial grounds) is certainly convenient for the capitalist, not least because it merges the supreme, historic reputation of Islam with the inferior, present reputation of capitalism.

As Max Weber rightly mentions, capitalism is not purely the desire to acquire wealth, it is a method to organise society.[4] Thus, the Islamic economy and the free market are clearly fractions of two different (and even opposing) ideological constructs, which hold certain fundamental ideas towards man, life and this universe. So one cannot selectively compare elements of two distinctly different economic systems and coalesce them together without contextualising their bases, as this would open the door to a number of inconsistencies. As primitive as it might seem, we find economists who attempt to pull thin strings from Islam and tie them to this system. It must be noted, Muhammad (ﷺ) neither advocated a free market when he allowed prices to fluctuate nor champion a command economy when he regulated the monopoly. In fact, he (through his message) brought the world a new form of economics.

Indeed, Islam is a comprehensive way of life and has a solution to all economic problems. Unlike capitalism, it is not an ideology fabricated in the meagre mind of man, for he (man) is inferior, limited and dependent. Consequently, any ideology that originates from him is flawed and or tainted with imperfection. In Islam, it is God who is supreme, unlimited and

Weber, 1905 [4]

independent and it is this position that forms the basis of the Islamic economic ideology. Thus Allah (ﷻ) is sovereign, He defines right from wrong and knows what is best for man, for He created him and will always remain the ultimate legislator.

Although the Islamic economy may share some features with other economic systems, it fundamentally differs from each of them. That is to say it does not resemble a free market system nor a command economy. Likewise, it is not an adaptation of any capitalist school of thought nor is it a form of mercantilism (merchant capitalism). Rather it is unique in structure and founded on radically different ideas. This should be the starting point of any comparative study; once we have successfully purged the mind of any presuppositions over what the Islamic economy 'shares' with other economic systems, we can subsequently progress with an impartial, comparative analysis between the Islamic economic system and capitalism.

FUNDAMENTALS OF THE FREE MARKET:

I. **The economic problem:** In classical theory, resources are assumed to be scarce within the market whilst demand for them is thought to be infinite. According to the capitalist, demand is a combination of both needs and wants. Thus man, by nature, has an infinite demand and will always expend effort to satisfy it through the pursuit of tangible and intangible goods. From this logic, it is clear that so long as capitalism produces more goods which satisfy the needs/wants of people, irrespective of what they are and their effects on society, the benefit from this satisfaction becomes a sufficient, yet necessary solution to the scarcity of resources and mans infinite demand.

The economic problem consequently becomes a basis for production; the larger the amount of goods and services endowed to man, the greater the extent to which his infinite demand is quenched. So capitalism is concerned primarily with indicators such as GDP (gross domestic product) and GNP (gross national product), as they indicate the value of how many goods and services that are produced in a given period of time. Thus, a higher gross domestic or national product indicates a greater extent to which the economic problem is being resolved. This is the central objective of capitalism and it is a matter threaded throughout the free market as we will later realise in the coming chapters.

II. **The primacy of price:** As a general and primitive concept, price is a crucial variable within any economic system. It effectively allocates resources through its intimacy with supply and demand. Economists call this phenomenon the 'price mechanism', where the supply and demand of goods/services are determined by the price level. The former positively, whilst the latter negatively.

Consumers who purchase good X, signal producers that there is a demand for it. An increase in consumer demand for this good pushes producers to raise the price for it and increase production due to the profit involved and to meet the excess demand. Likewise, a halt in the consumption of X, signals producers to cease production as there is no profit in producing such a good, due to a lack of demand. So individual agents determine themselves what should be produced and consumed within an economy based on price signals. Consequently, the supply and demand of these resources are connected within the free market through the price mechanism, and at an equilibrium they are allocated through a particular price and quantity (see appendix I).

Whilst there is unanimity over the price mechanism (due to its descriptive nature), capitalism considers it to be the sole regulator in distributing resources. Indeed, it is firmly believed by classical economists that the price mechanism attains economic equilibrium because society collectively organises itself to choose the necessities of production and consumption at any given point in time. This equilibrium indicates a point where the economy optimally produces what is demanded and vice versa. This concept (of the price mechanism attaining equilibrium through consumers and producers choosing for themselves what resources should circulate), is what Adam Smith famously coined as 'the invisible hands of the market'.[5] We can see that in capitalism, producers produce based on signals from the price mechanism and it is certainly this level of price that encourages agents to seek profit (as it is revenue for the producer and a cost for the consumer). According to the capitalist, it is only based on price signals and the price mechanism that all economic agents act upon or conform to, as they are purely material beings that seek material benefit. Price subsequently becomes the sole conversation, point of evaluation, incentive and even constraint, that motivates or prevents the economic man from attaining this material benefit. Free market economists claim that this behaviour epitomises the 'rational' nature of a human being, due to his ability to assess the market and make decisions based on price signals to maximise his utility.

III. **Value:** This principle is related to value although it also links into the aforementioned principle of price. The term 'value' connotes what goods and services are important to society; if a good is said to be high in value it means it is high in importance and vice versa. Value is a core measure for economic decision making as it is a measurement for exchange and benefit. A higher valued object can only be exchanged for something of its equivalence and the same concept applies for a lower valued object. The concept of value is the effective basis upon which human's observe goods and services, so as to make the correct decisions when producing, consuming and distributing. Money is therefore recognised as a container of value, a yardstick and a medium of exchange. However, under the capitalist frame of thought, value (the benefit of a thing to society) is often interpreted through the lens of price; the greater the price of an object, the more money one must forgo and it is generally thought that the higher price indicates a more profitable good or service. In other words, capitalism incentivises economic agents to observe value through the lucrative prism of price as opposed to innate worth.

---

[5] Smith, 1776

IV. **Freedom and ownership:** As a result of the Siècle des Lumières (Century of Enlightenment), the collapse of feudalism and a separation from the clergy, economists have regularly attributed economic freedom to success. This concept is endemic under liberal capitalism and it is a common belief that greater freedom leads to better decisions amongst economic agents, which ultimately leads to an improved economic system. Among the many rights of freedom that this ideology has endowed man, that which is cherished most is the freedom of ownership, which mainly manifests in the 'classical' roots of liberal capitalism. Some of the leading figures in this school of thought include Adam Smith, Alfred Marshall, David Ricardo, Thomas Malthus and John Stuart Mill. These economists generally believe that if the market is left to organise itself with full autonomy it will determine what is best for society. This is, according to most classical economists, the epitome of a perfectly 'free' market economy, whilst government intervention is generally considered a disturbance to the values of liberal capitalism and more importantly to the market's equilibrium.

V. **Rational choice theory and utility maximisation:** This principle fundamentally assumes man to be a rational creature that will always (by nature) seek to maximise his own personal utility. In essence, capitalism has secured the freedom for man to maximise his utility but has left the method to do so, amorphous and undefined. In other words, capitalism is less concerned with what direction society ought to move towards, and is more concerned with how it is functioning in the present, given the strong faith in man's rational nature. Neoclassical economists firmly believe in this form of behavioural economics as it is a principle that has been 'empirically' grounded upon countless experiments conducted by notable academics.[6]

These are some of the core ideas that drive capitalism. Whilst there are certainly other fundamental principles, it is clear that the five presented have immense weight in this discussion.

Jevons, 1871 [6]

<u>ISLAM'S REBUTTAL TO CAPITALISM:</u>

Rebutting principle I: There is a fundamental flaw behind this principle. It is the unification of two concepts that are dissimilar, such that when merged and considered as one, the focus of economic policy diverges and when implemented, pushes the error on to society. Capitalists were right to suggest that there is an economic problem but they failed miserably in their attempt to define what it is. They have formulated their viewpoint by chaining the concept of an infinite demand (without defining what this consists of) to the idea that there are limited means to satisfy it (which is a position, dependant on the former). Based on this erroneous principle, it is firmly believed that producing more will satisfy a greater demand although it can never quench it entirely.

However, there is a difference between what man requires and what he desires, that is to say his needs and wants. In addition to this, an improvement to an economy's productive capacity does not necessarily ensure an enhancement to distribution. This is the vital difference between the science of production and the system of distribution and it is a distinction that the capitalists have not made. As a result of amalgamating these two concepts, the free market inherited a rather serious issue.

Rebutting principle II: Although price is primarily linked to distribution, it is not the sole basis upon which economic agents behave. It is possible for producers to produce solely for the sake of good character or even on a spiritual basis. This definition of price restricts man to merely a material creature when in reality he can be motivated by other factors. So price is not the only incentive for production and consumption. When all goods and services conform to the subject of price, earning becomes a means of survival (in that humans must attain money to remain alive) rather than a route to comfort. This is yet another fallacy under the capitalist system as there is a lack of thought for those who are unable to attain capital through exerting effort. If (as it is) the price mechanism was the only autonomous method to distribute resources (all goods and services came under the subject price), the weak and the poor would not receive much whilst the rich and the wealthy would benefit and exploit the market. Those who are stronger and more capable, quick and inventive, smart and business minded are able to 'capitalise' on their skills and attain more wealth, allowing them to afford what is priced and valuable. However, those who cannot exert effort (even if that was due to a physical constraint) are looked at in contempt, their survival is insignificant and it is only due to the current morals held by society (which are constantly susceptible to change), that pressure governments to intervene and sustain them. In fact, only a minority of the destitute are cared for, whilst the rest are left to wither away. Today, we find many who even question the economy's role in catering for such people, as if they do not, as human beings, deserve to be kept alive.

Finally, the notion of an equilibrium may sound attractive in principle but it must not be used as a pretext for extensive deregulation. The economy is a dynamic organism that is constantly changing, hence the point of equilibrium within any market is always prone to shift from one place to another. Whilst such a movement is natural and some may argue inevitable, that is not to say the economy must remain entirely independent to correct itself, rather it may be necessary at times (just as Keynes once proved) for power to mix with the market, so as to achieve a better outcome for society/state.

Rebutting principle III: Capitalism equates value with price; the higher something is priced, the more valuable it is thought to be due to its profitability. We find this to be an axiom in almost every economy, yet it is a grave misjudgment of a key concept giving rise to serious problems like bubbles. Value is judged by how beneficial a thing is to society in satisfying the needs and wants of the people whilst also assessing its rarity. The error arises in pinning this to the concept of price. By doing so, people are pushed to look through the nominal as opposed to the real. If the price of a good increases, the value and or benefit of it does not alter. Value ought to be determined by observing the good's intrinsic value (within the market) and not purely by the profitability of its price. As a result of this incoherence, capitalism has yet another source of market failure by facing the opportunity costs of producing and perpetuating goods that are merely priced higher relative to those goods which are more valuable and beneficial to society.

Rebutting principle IV: Ultimate freedom and autonomy are dangerous concepts in any economic system, as they act as an incentive for man to peddle his selfish interests by any means necessary. Indeed, the idea of freedom itself is also defective by nature as it is a precursor to chaos and inefficiency as opposed to structure and success. Contrastingly, Islam maintains an economy in a particular fashion according to particular principles that do not alter, rather they are perfect in source and have been proven to consistently solve economic problems. It must be noted; man by nature is weak, limited and needy, additionally he is greedy and is swayed by the environment in which he operates. Capitalism has failed to understand that with full autonomy, agents lead economies into total anarchy whilst markets left to regulate themselves create deficiencies in the state's distributive function. The Islamic economic system regulates the market and leaves it to function where necessary (not due to the concept of freedom, which is the foundation for classical theory, but due to the order of Allah ﷻ).

Rebutting principle V: Human's are certainly rational beings but that is not to say they are inherently good decision makers that are capable of discerning right from wrong. Capitalism has been unsuccessful at identifying what society should look like, so as to regulate the manner in which human's make rational choices and improve their utility. As a result of this freedom and autonomy, ideas of profit maximisation and individual self-interest have filtered through to almost every facet of the global economy. This is a core problem, as agents are making rational choices purely based on factors such as profit and not the benefit to society. Due to this corruption, endemic failure has now plagued the roots of capitalist based markets resulting in poor wealth distribution. This misconception evidently stems from an incoherent understanding of humans and their nature.

In the Islamic economy, man is guided by the *sharia* in any effort to improve his utility. Furthermore, utility is not always seen through the prism of profit, but it also involves pleasing God. So Islam has an outlook on society and it regulates the economy accordingly. This viewpoint evidently contradicts the capitalist ideology, which holds no intrinsic belief towards what the economy ought to be, leaving man generally unregulated and free to wreak total havoc. Thus, ethics in Islam are not left to the wavering minds of men but established through time and determined by God Himself. In other words, there are no presuppositions which place a moral faith in man, but there is a perfect criteria according to which he is expected to operate.

PRINCIPLES OF THE ISLAMIC ECONOMIC SYSTEM[7]:

I. **The economic problem:** Unlike capitalism, the Islamic system understood demand to be finite (by virtue of its definition) and that there are enough resources to satisfy this limited demand. It focuses primarily on the possession of wealth rather than the growth an economy experiences.

    Given this principle, the Islamic economic system seeks to ensure the wellbeing of society through guaranteeing the basic necessities of every citizen within the state. It observes man first and foremost as a human being with human problems and survival instincts, before observing his desire for luxuries, which it also motivates him to satisfy. Islam does not intervene in matters relating to the economic science (productive capacity), so the economy is flexible in adopting new and innovative styles/means of production with the objective of improving growth.

    Contrary to popular belief, the Islamic economic system encourages this matter entirely, but it will always prioritise wealth distribution over capital accumulation and equity over an aggressive growth based mentality. In doing so, the economy paves the way for collective progression and higher sustainability in the long run.

II. **Acquisition, ownership and disposal of wealth:** Wealth fluidity is perhaps the most important problem in the Islamic economic system as it is directly related to the ease at which man is able to satisfy his needs and wants. Islam is concerned with ownership as it understood that humans have a natural propensity to generate wealth, whilst the economic problem actually arises when handling it. So the objective of the state is to facilitate the distribution of capital through organising the methods by which man possesses or comes into contact with it. In order to ensure a steady flow around the economy, policies aim to ensure that capital is properly acquired, disposed and transferred.

For example; capitalism champions private ownership, whilst Islam actively regulates the private sector in which capital is often inefficiently allocated and trapped. To reiterate the aforementioned point, whilst Islam emphasises the distribution of wealth, this is not to say that it ignores growth. Improving an economy's productive capacity is ultimately unavailing if new capital is unable to flow, allowing more to enjoy additional goods/services. By focusing on these three factors, Islam maximises the velocity and range at which wealth switches hands.

III. **Economic outlook:** The Islamic economic system is concerned with the relationship people have in society and so it holds a position on how the economy ought to manifest. In other words, Islam as a doctrine maintains the economy according to a specific criteria. Whilst capitalism is ignorant of many things attached with trade, Islam realises that humans in society interact when exchanging goods/services and consequently seeks to observe and manage the impact these relationships have on society itself. Thus the Islamic economic system maintains economic policies that specifically prohibit the exchange and usage of certain goods and services (in the public sphere), with the objective of preserving and protecting human interactions from what is rendered virulent to society by the Islamic *Aqeedah* (creed).

17

For example; the capitalist may look unto something as beneficial merely due to its demand and profitability, whilst Islam holds an entirely different outlook. That is to say it does not haphazardly conclude the benefit of a good based on the potential profit involved in producing and selling it (due to its ability to satisfy a need/want), rather it assesses the nature of the good/service and evaluates its real benefit within the market, after which it regulates its production and consumption accordingly.

IV. **Ideological concepts (behavioural economics):** Islamic concepts such as *rizq* (provisions), *taqwa* (piety/God consciousness), *al-qadaa wal qadar* (the divine decree), et cetera, have a massive influence on the entire economy that are often unexplained out of incapacity by the capitalist. Contrary to popular belief, those who subscribe to the Islamic ideology do not behave in line with ideas such as freedom, democracy and or liberalism, rather they act in accordance to the *sharia* and submit to nothing except the sovereignty of the Almighty. As we will go on to discuss at various stages within this book, each of these Islamic concepts are able to facilitate economic progression and even avert potential crises.

To conclude, these are the core principles that guide the Islamic economic system to prosperity and success. They construct a solid foundation which fortify and reinforce the economic framework with concrete strength. As this book develops, we will notice the manner in which each principle is intricately embedded within Islamic economic policy and how they operate in consonance with society.

III. INEQUALITY AND THE ECONOMIC PROBLEM

Synopsis: Capitalism has misunderstood the economic problem by amalgamating the science of production with the system of distribution. This conceptual error has subsequently produced endemic market failure and rampant capital inequality.

Inequality can be defined as the inefficient apportionment of wealth, assets and income. The cause of such inequity stems from a poor distributive system, which has created an immense disparity between the lower and upper echelon of society. This plague is endemic within the free market, such that the richest 1% currently own more than the 99% of us put together. Furthermore, this percentile is only comprised of roughly 62 individuals out of the worlds total population, all of whom hold the same amount of wealth as the bottom half of humanity (equivalent to roughly 3.6 billion people)![8]

Studies concerning inequality have consistently shown skewed statistics (particularly in respect to the Lorenz curve) when mapping out the worlds cumulative share of income against a fraction of its total population. In fact, the Gini coefficient/index/ratio (a statistical tool to assess income distribution and inequality) seems to be nearing one (complete inequality) and away from zero (complete equality), in both the developed and developing world, indicating a global trend of deteriorating capital inequality (see appendix II).[9]

Many economists have hitherto, overlooked the human cost of this problem. As a result of capital inequality, we find that the wealthier bracket of society have a higher life expectancy, better education, less social problems and an improved quality of life. Contrastingly, the lower bracket of society face issues from death to violence, imprisonment, high rates of illiteracy, low levels of life expectancy and a generally poor standard of living. Such polarity must not be trivialised to digits and statistics, rather it must be recognised as an endemic virus, affecting billions of real people around the world.

---

[8] Credit Suisse, 2014
[9] Piketty, 2014; Subacchi, 2016

Moreover, it must be treated with extreme urgency, so as to preserve life and its quality in the long run. These capital imbalances can only be explained by an immanent flaw within the current economic system. In order to locate the root cause, one must understand how capitalism has defined its 'economic problem', which is a prescriptive (normative) matter unique to all economic systems and can be defined as the underlying purpose that drives macroeconomic thought and action. Such an ideological concept is an indispensable matter in any economy, as it cascades through the entire economic system.

CAPITALISM'S PROBLEM OF SCARCITY:

The proponents of capitalism have insisted that man as a human being desires an infinite amount of goods and services. They have, upon this inference, deduced that there will never be enough resources to fulfil man's infinite desires. Capitalism's economic problem is therefore concerned with organising the capital that man already possesses, so as to ensure that society maximises its utility. Economist Paul Samuelson first outlined this issue in three fundamental questions; the first was concerned with what goods/services society should produce, the second focused on how society should use their resources to facilitate this production and the third concentrated on whom they should be produced for.[10] Together, these questions form capitalism's economic problem, which is to maximise societies utility with a limited supply of scarce resources.

To simplify this concept, one may use the analogy of a vessel, in which some of the worlds resources exist. According to the capitalist theory, man consumes the whole vessel only to demand more due to his infinite thirst. The questions that naturally follow from this 'rational' observation are as follows: What should one include or omit in this vessel? How should one use his resources to produce these goods and who amongst society should have access to them? In response, capitalism has suggested that the greater the amount of resources made available to man by way of production, the greater the extent to which the state can satisfy his infinite demand.

Samuelson, 1947; Smith 1776 [10]

As a result of such an understanding, the free market revolves around the concept of growth, for it is the act of producing more, which settles the economic problem. In other words; a higher productive capacity expands the supply of goods available to man, thus quenching more of his (albeit infinite) demand. Therefore, a higher level of production is invaluable to the capitalist; it is a means to increase GDP, a signal of economic stimulation and an attestation that more demand (albeit infinite) is being met. We see the practical manifestation of this conceptual conviction within the contemporary economy, where gross domestic product (GDP) and gross national product (GNP) are considered two of the main indicators which determine economic success. Unsurprisingly, both are concerned only with the value of production within the domestic and international economy.

In the midst of this growth imperative, mankind has realised a paradox; the rich have access to resources that the poor can only dream of and that the upper echelon of society bathe in the fruits of increased production whilst the lower class must scrounge for their leftovers. It seems then, that capitalism is a system incessantly preoccupied with growth but simultaneously insouciant towards distributing its resources. In refuting such a paradox, many free market economists often raise Pareto's principle of optimality as a justification to the omnipresence of inequality. It states that one man's gain is another man's loss and that no one man can be better off except at the expense of another. Thus according to the capitalist, inequality must be tamed through excessive production, so as to increase the amount of capital that is distributed to society.

However, there is an assumption here that everyone in society shares the same cake (capital) providing they employ enough effort to attain a slice. In reality, the rich and those with power are the only class who possess a portion whilst the poor had no seat at the table to begin with. Upon further inspection, one would realise that the solution is not to enlarge the cake for the rich to feast on, rather it is to distribute each slice to society so that every man equally gains and none are worse off, which is known as a 'Pareto improvement'. With this in mind, we find that the indicators (GNP/GDP) used to determine economic prosperity are measures of productive capacity, but they tell economists little about the possession of capital and how it is filtered in society, which is a matter that pertains to an economy's distributive function. We often observe politicians and economists alike in a constant struggle to increase these indicators but as we have seen, it may be that they are impressive whilst the economy suffers from mass poverty due to rampant inequality. It may also be that the capitalist meets the needs of a few people through excessive production, only to forsake the majority who are devoid of basic necessities. So I ask the reader; what is the opulence of an economy thereafter?

ISLAM'S PROBLEM OF INEQUITY:

To begin, the Islamic economic system's prime objective is to fulfil man's basic necessities. It must be noted; the one who does not differentiate the needs of man from his wants, has failed to understand the purpose of an economic system in its entirety. If we observe the human condition, we find that man naturally prioritises, that is to say he does not demand an expensive vehicle when he has no food to eat nor does he demand a gold palace when he has no clothes to wear. Thus, man as a human being fundamentally demands basic goods and services, which his survival depends on, all before he demands luxury goods. In other words, he first seeks to secure his needs (food/clothing/shelter) before securing his wants. These basic demands are not infinite but finite and quantifiable, which is in stark contrast to the economic imperative we know of today.

Such an observation is the foundation for Islam's viewpoint towards the economic problem and it is a concept that radically alters the current mode of thought. Whilst we notice the error in amalgamating these needs with the wants of man, that is not to say the latter is fictitious within the subject of demand. The point of this distinction is to understand that luxuries in life are not sought when necessities have not yet been attained, hence the latter should be prioritised over the former.

In fact, the Islamic economic system has meticulously detailed the components of this demand and the importance for the state to guarantee it for every citizen by way of textual evidence:

Muhammad (ﷺ) is reported to have said that "*the son of Adam has no better right than that he would have a house wherein he may live, a piece of clothing whereby he may hide his nakedness and a piece of bread and some water.*"[11]

Therefore, if man as a human being has a limited demand for goods and services (i.e. basic necessities) then what of our ability to quench it? Indeed, after assessing the global economy, one must certainly conclude that the world harbours enough resources to sufficiently fulfil man's immediate demand. So the issue is not about quantity per se, rather about distribution. In other words, the economic system need not focus entirely on the production of capital, for mankind already possesses or is in the same domain which contains an abundance of it. Rather, what is required by the economic system is to focus on distributing this wealth, so as to ensure every man's basic necessities have been met. Only then will an economy truly be successful in managing the wealth of its people.

Islam is the only ideology that maintains an economy whose primary concern is the system of economic distribution as opposed to the science of economic growth. Hence most problems under capitalism are intimately linked to phenomena such as inequality and allocative inefficiency, whilst it clearly excels in areas such as productivity/technological progress. However, poor capital diffusion is inherent to the free market and so long as capitalism remains, those who try to resolve the issue will be forever trapped in a vicious cycle of economic recidivism. As many studies have shown, concentrating capital within small clusters of society is unsustainable in the long run as activity only occurs in the realm where the rich benefit. Capital redistribution has hence become the only route to reducing pervasive inequity and it is Islam that acts in such a manner. In fact, by redefining the economic problem, society gains from Islam, what capitalism has failed to deliver.

---

[11] At-Tirmidhi, ND; Abu Dawud, ND

One must not take this principle (of distribution) as the sole objective of the Islamic economic system, rather one should recognise its priority over growth. Islam also focuses on the economic sciences and unlike the system of distribution, it is open to adopt and or refine methods to increase productivity. Contrary to popular belief Islam was at the pinnacle of technological advancement and economic growth. From the works of Ibn Khurdādhbih to Al-Bīrūnī, Ibn Sīnā to Al-Khwārizmī, Ibn al-Haytham to Omar Khayyám, the Muslims were the vanguards of scientific and technological progression, which is an elemental component of economic expansion as it facilitates both production (growth) and distribution.[12]

In fact, let us not forget, that it was Adam smith himself who once said: "...*the empire of the Caliphs seems to have been the first state under which the world enjoyed that degree of tranquility which the cultivation of the sciences requires. It was under the protection of those generous and magnificent princes, that the ancient philosophy and astronomy of the Greeks were restored and established in the East; that tranquility, which their mild, just and religious government diffused over their vast empire, revived the curiosity of mankind, to inquire into the connecting principles of nature.*"[13]

Finally, the means through which such an end (of effective distribution) is achieved can be found throughout this book as opposed to merely this specific chapter, which is primarily a theoretical explication of Islam's economic imperative. The practical ramifications of such cognition will become clear as we progress, particularly in terms of Islamic economic policy.

Alkhateeb, 2014 [12]
Smith, 1869 [13]

IV. IMPERFECT COMPETITION

Synopsis: *Firms and businesses with unrestricted autonomy to manipulate the price mechanism, is what ultimately skews the market for goods and services. Such power has given rise to monopolies, oligopolies and highly imperfect competition.*

In the 19th century, capitalism began to witness frequently emerging markets that were controlled entirely by single firms and or individuals. For example, men like John D. Rockefeller took almost all profits in the rising market for oil after he set up the monopolist 'Standard Oil', which controlled 88% of refined flows in the US and 91% of total production.[14] As a result of Western imperialism, new commodities were gradually being introduced into developed capitalist economies, giving many agents thereafter a lucrative incentive to hoard the supply of particular inputs, so as to monopolise the market.

The British company DeBeers exemplified this phenomena. It monopolised the market for diamonds by controlling mines discovered from colonial invasions in 1988. With a market share of 80%-90% it gained supernormal profits by charging extremely high prices for diamonds.[15] In reaction to the monopoly surge of the early 20th century, economies began to enforce competition policies such as the Sherman Act of 1890 and the Clayton Act of 1914. These canons ultimately aimed to strip firms of their market power, pave the way for equitable prices, improve the supply for monopolised commodities and reinstate a competitive environment within affected markets.[16]

Over a century later, capitalism still fosters a number of highly competitive firms that are superpowers in their industry. It seems that policies introduced in the latter part of the 20th century (such as the Competition Act of 1998) have had little impact on regulating imperfectly competitive markets. In fact, we even find certain patent and copyright laws that actually assist monopolies to grow even larger in size and market power.

---

[14] Times, 1937
[15] Goldschein, 2011
[16] Posner, 1976

The monopolisation of key resources such as oil, technology, energy and healthcare, has skewed resource distribution and produced a high level of opportunity costs. Before we seek a solution to monopolies, we must first dissect them, so as to understand their nature and how they emerge.

MONOPOLIES AND MARKET SOVEREIGNTY:

In the study of economics, price is firmly linked to distribution, insofar as it is the indicator observed by both producers and consumers to effectively make economic decisions in order to attain the most efficient outcome. However, this mechanism can be exploited in an economy where firms and industries are granted high levels of autonomy to maximise profits. Indeed, in a case where price is the sole regulator for distribution, liberal capitalism enables the elevation of firms and businesses to an echelon where they are able to regulate this regulator and command prices rather than take them as the market sets them to be. This occurs due to a large share of market power, which permits firms/businesses to dictate market movements merely by setting the price of their goods and services.

Monopolies are a core example of a failure within the market, that is to say a failure in allocating resources efficiently. As we will see, issues that stem from an unregulated market can have many repercussions, such that without intervention the rich and powerful are able to manipulate the price mechanism in order to attain supernormal profits at the expense of the destitute. In this regard, monopolies are often born from the possession of scarce resources or rare goods. In most cases, governments bestow firms the power to become a monopolist through the control of particular resources. In fact, it is common for governments themselves to monopolise the market so as to direct profit into political devices or private corporations in order to fund specific interests. These muscular entities have the autonomy to exploit scarce resources, enjoy super normal profits, close the doors to other competitors (due to high barriers to entry) and charge exorbitant prices, all of which have a negative impact on market surplus.

As the price mechanism is the main regulator for distribution, monopolies also skew the allocation of resources, primarily because of the prices they set (by virtue of the market power they hold). Such pricing is an extremely popular option for imperfect competitors, as it increases their revenue, particularly when demand for the monopolise good is inelastic. These entities also tend to lower their supply (at times iniquitously), ultimately reducing the consumption of goods/services that are often highly inelastic, which can deprive a society of important resources. An example of this is the monopolisation of core energy such as oil or basic resources like coal, salt, petroleum, utilities, transport, medicine, healthcare, et cetera.

As a result of rising prices and underproduction within the market, monopolies shrinks consumer surplus and generate what is known as 'dead weight loss', which is essentially the measure of what is lost in respect to society's well being (see appendix III). Further still, this lack of supply and strong competition often contributes to higher rates of unemployment within the labour market, leading to greater levels of inequality. Evidently then, monopolies are a virulent source of market failure and a poisonous phenomenon in society. They have, however, become a norm under the free market, primarily due to the values of liberal capitalism. The omnipresence of such an ideology within society has incentivised agents to maximise their profit by exploiting the market wherever and whenever they see fit. To make matters even worse, this unscrupulous mentality is kindled by capitalism's deregulatory predilection.

That being said, many attempts have been made to resolve the negative externalities created in a monopoly, but they involve a temporary remedy rather than a permanent fix. Indeed, here we must differentiate the reactionary from the preventative; to purge the problem of imperfect competition, one must address capitalism's principles, so as to prevent this issue from occurring in the first instance. However, seldom do we see such thought, instead, governments often make use of temporary solutions to correct market failure through policies like price ceilings, price floors and quantity regulations.

Finally, monopolists under the capitalist state is not an issue per se, rather the concern is when firms abuse market power to an extent where the burden on consumers and other competitors overrides the material benefit to the economy. Of course, this is a paradox because monopolies are generally a hindrance to society by nature. To this end, let the negative effects associated with them be a sufficient reason for their destruction.

Islam acts in such a manner by prohibiting monopolies entirely, primarily through preventative means as opposed to enacting reactionary policy. In other words, Islam does not allow for a monopoly to foster within the market only to later regulate it. In fact, Islamic economic policy makes it extremely difficult for a monopoly to arise naturally, rather it would have to be a product of force or further still, an act of cheating the market.

On the issue of market sovereignty through excessive power, the Messenger of Allah (ﷺ) is reported to have said, that '*no one monopolises except the wrongdoer*' and in another similar narration, that '*whoever monopolised is a wrongdoer*.'[17]

ISLAMIC MARKET STRUCTURE POLICY:

I.   **Ending copyrights, patents and IP rights:** Whilst the rights of owning tangible goods such as trademarks are protected, the concept of intellectual property rights is foreign to Islam. It prevents people from procuring inventions/discoveries with the objective of developing them further by giving owners the incentive to hoard, so as to remain a monopolist over their production. To eliminate this phenomenon, firms and industries should be relatively transparent. This lucidity ultimately paves the way for competition within the market as it reduces barriers to entry. In fact, contrary to popular belief, the removal of intellectual property rights can certainly benefit society, as it enables others to freely advance resources and technology, rather than constantly having to overcome boundaries in order to progress.

---

28   Al-Bukhari, ND; Ibn al-Hajjaj, ND [17]

This is a massive hindrance for many under capitalism as barriers to entry are excessively high, deterring firms and businesses from technological and scientific innovation, consequently stunting development. Such a profit maximising predisposition is particularly evident within the industry for patents, in which there are cases being filed for products that are yet to exist! Such chaos is a clear indication of how agents in capitalism do not operate to propel society forward as a collective entity, rather they behave upon opportunistic egocentricity, so as to reap the entire market of its benefit.

There is a belief held by many that suggests intellectual property rights actually encourage innovation due to the security of potential profit. One must understand that this only occurs in an economy grounded upon a profit maximisation mentality, with little care for the impact to society. Islamic economic policy would redefine such thinking with the concept of collective progression. Indeed, such restriction secures profit for the few and leaves the many worse off whilst Islam works to ensure that the many are better off with the inventions of a few. By removing copyright, patent and intellectual rights, society is able to expand the boundaries for technology and science, even further than capitalism has.

II. **Preventing privatisation:** Most monopolies arise from the control of natural resources or even basic goods like water, natural gas and electricity. In Islam, such goods are owned by the public sector and the state does not permit their privatisation, thus removing any possibility for corporations to hoard a given resource. Furthermore, these firms and businesses can be dangerous as they seize market power rapidly due to the inelastic nature of the supply they hoard. Islam does not impose a price for public goods, as they belong to the people and the state has no right to use these matters as a source of revenue except from managing them on behalf of the public.

III. **Modulating market power:** A monopoly occurs when there is only one firm in the market of a good or resource. Under an Islamic economy, markets would be regulated and monitored to level competition so that one single firm does not own the entire supply of a valuable good. Islam obliges the state to strip firms and businesses of their power if necessary. On this matter, capitalist governments often give agents the power and means to monopolise a market for their own economic interests; contrastingly, the Islamic economic system rejects the concept of a monopoly altogether and would certainly prevent it from manifesting in any shape or form.

IV. **Proscribing price-fixing:** Monopolies are able to assess elasticities and adjust prices accordingly, so as to accrue supernormal profits. Governments can also fix price ceilings and floors to regulate a monopoly or even the market in general. Contrastingly, in an Islamic economy it is generally forbidden to tamper with the price mechanism unless such policy is necessary to safeguard the people's basic necessities.

To manage inconsistencies within the market, the state would often make use of quantity regulations (such as quotas, et cetera). However, economic policy would primarily focus on the actions and or environment that causes the price mechanism to falter in the first instance, thus preventing a skew in resource allocation.

On this specific matter (price regulation), Anas (may Allah be pleased with him) narrated that the price level once rose at the time of Muhammad (ﷺ), so they (the companions) said to him: "*O Messenger of Allah, we wish you would price (fix the prices)*." He replied: "*Indeed Allah is the Creator, the holder, the Open-handed, the Provider, the Pricer; and I wish I will meet Allah and nobody demands (complains) of me for an unjust act I did against him, neither in blood or property.*"[18]

Ibn-Hanbal, ND [18]

V. **Preventative policy:** Under the Islamic economic model, firms and businesses are all subject to economic policies and regulations within society that act to neutralise imperfect competitors before they rise to power. Early indication of a monopoly is suppressed by the state as a preventative measure rather than letting the issue manifest and tackling it later in a reactionary manner. As we have clearly seen, monopolies are a threat to the economy's employment, supply and pricing. So taking care of this issue before it arises can prevent the harm that is associated with imperfect competition in the long run.

It may be difficult at this point for the reader to conceive of a model in which such competition can be understood and further still, what impact such policy has on the market at large. However, it must be noted, that economic models are merely an explication of reality and not a source of it. In other words, whilst they do not necessarily produce outcomes, economic models certainly explain phenomena. Therefore, as the reality of such competition is yet to exist, it becomes difficult to construct a mathematical and graphical representation of what these markets would potentially look like. That being said, one can, at this point, refer to classical theory for descriptive models on competition (particularly perfect and monopolistic), in which most markets under the Islamic economic system could potentially fit in (see appendix IV).

In such an instance, it is certainly permissible in Islam for the Muslim scholar to use these particular models as an analytical basis, for they are not driven by what is normative, rather grounded upon what is objective. This is the key difference between prescriptive and descriptive economics, whereby the Muslim is able to observe and adopt the latter but must entirely reject the former, providing it is based upon man-made thinking that is inferior to the legislation of Allah (ﷻ). This integral principle is found even within the books of *fiqh* and must be understood so as to discern what one is able to take, from what one must leave in contemporary economic theory.

After the implementation of such policy, one would expect to see positive results. Lower barriers to entry would invite more competition, which tends to neutralise imperfections within the market. As a result, consumer surplus would rise and the dead weight loss would diminish. This makes the economy better off as society is able to enjoy certain goods and services that would have been lost otherwise to a monopolist. Economies would also experience more technological advancement, primarily as a result of competitive innovation, which would only occur after the abolishment of patent/copyright/intellectual laws.

To conclude, this chapter has demonstrated how a monopoly arises and the adverse effects associated with highly imperfect competition. It has also presented an alternative (both in theory and in policy) to common market structures under the capitalist system by extirpating any form of highly imperfect competition through preventative measures. Thus Islam, unlike capitalism, ensures a healthy level of competition within a market that is much more effective in resource allocation.

V. INFLATION AND CURRENCY

Synopsis: At the heart of capitalism's financial infection lies the virus of the fiat currency. Its manipulation has given birth to business cycles, inflation and rapidly declining currency value.

On the 15th of August 1971, President Richard Nixon, under the influence of John Keynes, made a unilateral decision to halt convertibility between the dollar and gold, effectively paving the way for a new international monetary order, namely the 'fiat system', whose primary quality was a floating, as opposed to a fixed exchange rate. Before 'The Nixon Shock', which ultimately put an end to the Bretton Woods system, the nominal price of gold (not adjusted for inflation) seldom fluctuated and remained relatively stable, particularly due to its rigid supply and monetary inflexibility. However, post 1971, the USD ($) began to fall precipitously in value, whilst the price of gold rose dramatically at a similar rate, peaking at approximately $1,900 (oz t) in 2011 and roughly $1,200 (oz t) in 2015.[19]

Upon inspection, many often conclude that gold has merely appreciated over time, but as one is priced in the other, it is actually the fiat currency that has depreciated due to perennial monetary inflation. In fact, the fiat system has induced far more financial volatility than it once sought to control, primarily in the form of rapid depreciation and a subsequent rise in the average consumer price level. Such phenomena are a result of the fiat's flexibility and lack of intrinsic value, which has incentivised both the public and private sector to exploit its supply through expansionary monetary policy.

Inflation itself can be both beneficial and harmful depending on the economic climate, but persistently rising prices due to a mismatch in currency and growth do not bode well for any economy, particularly if they are outpacing nominal incomes. To critically analyse the macroeconomic effects of inflation and the fiat currency we must first understand both concepts in detail, for only then can we begin to seek their antidote.

---

[19] Macrotrends, 2015

INFLATION AND FIAT MONEY:

Inflation can be defined as a sustained increase in the price level within an economy over a given period of time. It is often measured by the annual percentage change in the Consumer Price Index (CPI). In the short run, low levels of inflation are understood to be caused by fluctuating demand and supply side factors involving both goods and services. Whereas in the long run, rising prices are attributed to money growth that is faster than the increase in gross domestic product. This chapter shall therefore focus on the latter, as opposed to short run fluctuations brought about by exogenous shocks in aggregate demand and or supply, which can be resolved through policy.

For centuries, the effects of both rising and falling prices have perplexed the most prolific economic minds this world has ever seen. However, it seems that over recent years, particularly after the inception of fiat money, this discussion has attracted even more heat. This is because, unlike its predecessor, fiat money has exacerbated the effects of a change in price on the overall economy, making it necessary for economists to try and mitigate phenomena such as inflation and or deflation. In fact, one could argue that the fiat system was the natural culmination of capitalism's principles, and that the natural transition from a commodity backed currency to an intrinsically worthless one was capitalism manifesting itself in its means of exchange.

The sources of inflation can be split into the following:

I.   **Demand-pull**: This term essentially refers to a difference between aggregate demand and aggregate supply. When demand in an economy rises (due to an increase in either consumption, investment, expenditure or net exports) and supply rises less than proportionally or stays the same, then the economy faces a mismatch. As a result of this imbalance between the aggregate demand and supply of goods, the entire economy must raise its prices to achieve an equilibrium (see appendix V).

II. **Cost-push**: This is when firms and businesses in an economy face higher production costs due to an increase in wages, resource prices, taxation, et cetera. As a result, agents raise prices to compensate for lower productivity. If demand is constant and productivity declines, this mismatch would produce inflation (see appendix V).

III. **Monetary**: This occurs due to a rapid growth in the money supply. When the stock of money rises faster than the output of an economy, there are too many notes chasing too few goods. The more cash people have, the higher their demand, causing prices to rise (see appendix V). Rightly so, most economists regard this as the main source for inflation, whilst the aforementioned are often considered negligible and or natural phenomenon.

The main problems associated with inflation are as follows[20]:

I. **Taxation**: Inflation can erode real purchasing power, providing it outpaces nominal wages, that is to say if real wages fall. In other words, when prices rise, consumers must part with more money to purchase the same quantity. Whilst it is vital to abstain from the inflation fallacy, one must recognise that if wages and inflation do not alter in tandem, then the latter would have an impact on purchasing power. Most classical economists are often nonchalant about this issue, primarily due to the theory of money neutrality, which states that rising prices have little impact on the real economy. However, this is not always true, in fact most economists now believe money is only neutral in the long run due to issues such as price and wage stickiness (monetary disequilibrium theory).

II. **Shoeleather costs**: These are essentially the opportunity costs of time and energy that result from constantly having to counter the effects of inflation by holding less money, that is to say by saving it in the bank (particularly in the form of bonds which give the saver a return).

---

[20] Mankiw and Taylor, 2014

III.   **Menu costs**: Most firms and businesses must change their prices frequently (so as to mitigate inflation) and are reluctant to do so, primarily due to the costs involved. Some of these costs involve printing new price listings and or catalogues, advertising new deals and even managing confusion and anger amongst consumers.

IV.   **Misallocation of resources**: Markets rely heavily on prices to allocate resources. Thus, any volatility in the price level ultimately interrupts the market's ability to distribute resources efficiently, which is a direct result of distorted decisions made by agents based on price signals.

V.   **Confusion and inconvenience**: Inflation disrupts the price mechanism, which can provoke judgment issues amongst economic agents. For example; investors are often unable to progress with certain projects due to an uncertainty in return whilst consumers may shift their behaviour (in consumption) due to confusion and a potential loss, which both incur costs to the economy.

VI.   **Hyperinflation**: This is a phenomenon in which prices are increasing rapidly due to uncontrolled money growth. During the post-war period (specifically 1946), Hungary experienced hyperinflation at 4.19×10^{16}%, which meant that prices were doubling every 15.3 hours.[21] Although somewhat rare, history has shown that many economies have, at some point in time, suffered from hyperinflation.

In fact, economists have actually altered the manner in which consumer prices are calculated, subsequently depressing inflation to a deceptively low level. This is certainly concerning, as hyperinflation is a virulent threat and can even be a precursor to crises, which was evident in Germany between 1921 and 1924.[22] Prices were said to be so volatile that people who went to restaurants paid before they sat to eat, for by the time they had finished the cost of what they ate would have risen significantly!

Thornton, 2015 [21]
C.R, 2013 [22]

VII. **Erosion**: When prices rise, the real value of household savings fall. As for those funds that are placed in the banking/financial sector in form of deposits/investment, in order for savings to maintain the same value, the inflation rate must equal to the interest rate. As this principle is not always consistent, rising prices often erode savings and the value of what is invested.

VIII. **Deflation**: Whilst inflation is generally harmful, deflation is often thought to be even worse. This phenomenon can be described as the antithesis of inflation and involves a persistent reduction in the price level over a given time period of time (see appendix VI). Declining prices are purported to severely damage the economy (due to real wage unemployment, a paradox of thrift, et cetera), however there are many erroneous myths attached to deflation that this chapter will go on to discuss.

Evidently then, inflation and deflation are naturally occurring phenomena when shifts in the money supply occur. At times when there is an excess of currency (that is to say the stock of money rises), prices also rise proportionally. Contrastingly, when there is a lack of currency (that is to say the stock of money falls) the price level also declines proportionally. Thus the question naturally becomes; what is the most efficient means of exchange and how does it operate to engender and or suppress inflation and or deflation?

Whilst economic history is dominated by some form of commodity backed currency, industrial capitalism has only recently introduced a monetary system whose legal tender is unbacked fiduciary paper or 'fiat money'. The benefit of such a regime is the freedom it gives to monetary authorities to float their currency and manipulate its supply so as to mitigate other economic problems (such as anaemic aggregate demand, unemployment, et cetera). However, as we know, monetary expansion ultimately puts pressure on the price level, which consequently reduces the unit value of money.

With the exception of a few, most monetary economists are seldom apprehensive about depreciation due to persistently rising prices, primarily due to the long (as opposed to short) term effects on the economy. However, it was this type of thinking that lead to the gold standard's demise, whereby economists began to focus purely on short run solutions to long run problems. The overwhelming desire to replace the gold standard with a fiat currency has had many ramifications for the international political economy, the greatest of which was perhaps the tradeoff between short run price instability under the Bretton Woods system and long run depreciation and price volatility under the contemporary fiat system.

As for the latter, the immense growth of credit has caused many to lose great confidence in the very cornerstone of their economic system; its currency. Despite the harsh, long run impact on monetary value, the problem of inflation is primarily related to the nature of the fiat itself. Indeed, if one were to blame rising prices on those who managed fiat money one would be attacking the symptom as opposed to the root cause. It is therefore incumbent to focus on the disposition of currency itself and by extension the monetary system it gives rise to. As such, the following subtopics will essentially make a strong case against the fiat and provide arguments for an alternative, namely the bimetallic standard (of gold and silver).

DISADVANTAGES OF THE FIAT SYSTEM:

I. **Depreciation**: Fiat money is intrinsically worthless, as it is not pegged to any physical commodity or real asset. This is an important issue because an unbacked currency is prone to manipulation (in terms of its supply). In fact, this is an endemic phenomenon under capitalism, peddled by the principles of profit and utility maximisation, which has severely depreciated fiat money since its inception (the dollar for example has lost approximately 97% of its value relative to gold)[23], leaving countries that adopt it, more vulnerable. Thus the fiat currency has become the epitome of a weak container of value and confidence.

Weiner, 2014 [23]

II. **Inflation**: As we have clearly seen, increasing the money supply through expansionary monetary policy, forces the price of goods and services to rise - providing these funds make their way into the private sector. Furthermore, the mismatch in currency supply relative to economic growth and trade has also generated inflationary pressures within the economy. The effects of inflation have been discussed extensively in the aforementioned sub-topic.

III. **Purchasing power**: Currency depreciation has led to a titanic reduction in consumer purchasing power (as inflation is outpacing nominal incomes, that is to say real incomes have fallen). A higher money supply essentially means that there are more notes chasing the same good. To combat this, the price of goods and services inevitably rise and consumers are left with a lower valued currency. The rapid decline in purchasing power has ultimately caused many agents (such as consumers and investors) to lose confidence in the currency itself. Such volatility has ultimately skewed trade; as subverting the medium of exchange is akin to subverting the exchange itself.

IV. **Business cycles**: Fiat currency is one of the underlying variables behind a business cycle and its link to inflation causes fluctuations in economic growth. These cycles can be represented by graphs that map out the movements of gross domestic product time. They are characterised by expansions and contractions, where an expansion is a period of sustained economic growth and a contraction is one of economic decline. The fiat is therefore a source (amongst others) of business cycles - a particular link we will discuss extensively in the next chapter.

PURPORTED ADVANTAGES OF THE FIAT SYSTEM:

I. **Monetary flexibility**: Many believe that the fiat currency is an excellent tool to moderate price issues (such as inflation and deflation) within the market. However, this is a red herring, as it is the manipulative nature of the fiat currency itself, that produces rising prices. Therefore, fiat money is a solution to its very own problem. In light of such a paradox, it is only rational to remove the currency altogether, so as to cure the problem as a whole.

II. **Business cycles**: In neo-classical theory controlling the money supply is considered a method by which the business cycle's busts can be corrected and booms can be extended. So according to most economists (specifically keynesian and monetarists), a fiat system is more useful than any commodity backed currency due to the ease at which the central bank can create credit. For the sake of this point we must briefly discuss the business cycle.

The 'bust' phase is often characterised by an economic recession in which unemployment is high, investment is low and the overall economy is contracting in terms of growth. Both governments and central banks try to combat this scenario through monetary and fiscal measures such as open market-operations (which involve quantitative easing), reducing interest rates, increasing expenditure, et cetera. Whilst these policies may be to correct the bust, they can introduce yet another recession after full employment has been achieved. This argument stems from a wider debate on why cycles occur altogether and specifically from an Austrian perspective.

However, whilst there may be some debate over what factors engender a cycle, history has shown that the manipulation of credit to reduce interest rates (so as to stimulate aggregate demand), has certainly produced unsustainable price bubbles in the short run, that have triggered recessions when realised. It is clear in this contemporary context, that the fiat is not a remedy to economic downturns, rather it is the reason why central banks are able to engage in the practice (of expanding credit), which ultimately leads to the very issue it is purported to resolve (of contracting liquidity and credit).

Evidently, there is a structural flaw within the capitalist framework. Many have insisted that the business cycle is a phenomenon ubiquitously present in all markets, but on the contrary we realise and as Karl Marx theorised, that 'creative destruction' is rather specific to capitalism. The argument that follows from this assumption, is that if one is to fix the omnipresent boom and bust cycle, one must use a manipulative currency to quell the problem in the short run, rather than using a fixed standard and waiting for delayed adjustment. However, such a solution produces cyclical results and in fact, it is the basis upon which the problem arose. The paradox here is clear; capitalism cannot remedy such a phenomenon, without giving birth to it again. In order to truly put an end to bust and boom, economies must adopt a stronger currency with intrinsic value and couple this with effective policy.

III. **Maintenance**: Some purport that it is cheap to maintain the fiat due to the minimal costs involved in expanding its supply. Whilst other currencies (such as those backed by a commodity) are much more costly to maintain due to mining and minting. However we must ask; relative to what? The cons of fiat money are beyond the mere discussion of maintaining it, indeed if it had brought the economy stability then this point would have some substance but the nature of such a currency is that it is incurring more costs to society than the central bank and governments are to save by maintaining it.

To resolve these issues, one must adopt a superior, more stable currency, immune to manipulation and effective in containing value. It seems that the antithesis of a worthless currency (a quality that engenders each of the aforementioned issues), is a commodity backed system. In this respect, the bimetallic (gold and silver) standard is an excellent alternative to the capitalist's fiat system and it is no surprise that the Islamic system mandates it. Let us analyse this monetary system, so as to conclude which is more effective; the fiat that is proposed by capitalism or the bimetallic standard mandated by Islam.

It must be noted, some of the following points are based on an assumption that gold is an international standard as opposed to a domestic currency. Indeed, I truly do believe that Thiers' Law will run its course once the gold standard returns and reigns supreme over the fiat, which will be discarded by the global economy. This is to say, antithetical to Gresham's law; good money will drive out the bad. For simplicity, this chapter will focus primarily on the gold standard as opposed to both metals.

ADVANTAGES OF THE GOLD STANDARD:

I.   **Value**: Gold is a precious metal, and is innately valued by society. It is a fixed currency and any paper money or coins within the economy would be backed by it. The percentage of backing is entirely dependant on the system in question, however Islam offers a rate of 100%. Hence this currency is stable and not prone to rapid depreciation, unlike the fiat, whose quantity is regularly exploited.

II.   **Exchange**: A stable currency is just as effective when translated onto the foreign exchange market. Given that exchange rates are fixed under a gold standard, currencies would be essentially fluctuate in sync. For example, if growth in C_A increased, this would push prices down (as gold is often fixed in the short run), making exports cheaper and more attractive to C_B, whilst simultaneously making imports more expensive and unattractive for C_A, ultimately creating a balance-of-payments surplus. This means that gold specie would flow from C_B to C_A, increasing the money supply in C_A, reversing the initial fall in prices and attaining a net balance. Such stability in exchange propels international trade with clarity, rather than engendering uncertainty amongst buyers and sellers.

III. **Security**: As money is backed by gold it is attached to the real economy and fixed by a physical quantity of specie and or bullion. Agents are therefore unable to perform credit creation at all, which ultimately secures consumer purchasing power and prices in the long run.

IV. **Long run price stability**: Under the historical classical gold standard, inflation was often rare or suppressed, due to a stable money supply. It is well documented that between 1880 and 1914, inflation under this monetary system within the United States, averaged a mere 0.1% per year. This is not to say that there would be no price instability under the gold standard, rather it is certainly infrequent over the long run. Besides, inflation is only virulent when it is high and unstable, in fact, a low level can even be beneficial. A gold standard would therefore improve economic decision making with price stability.

V. **Business cycles**: A gold currency extirpates the business cycle (assuming an endogenous origin). In switching to a commodity backed currency, economies waiver their right to expand the supply of credit (so as to push interest rates artificially down), with the objective of pumping up unsubstantiated gross domestic product in the short term only to subsequently face a bust. In other words, the gold standard paves the way for a more effective monetary structure, which will deter cycles.

VI. **Reputation**: Finally, the bimetallic system has a historical record of efficiency (particularly under the Islamic economic system). It existed for many centuries before the dollar was rendered a fiat currency in 1971 by the infamous Bretton Woods Agreement, which ultimately precipitated the aforementioned issues we see today.

PURPORTED DISADVANTAGES OF THE GOLD STANDARD:

I. **Monetary Rigidity**: The gold standard is often accused of being monetarily rigid, due to its fixed supply. Whilst it is true that fixed exchange rates make monetary policy ineffective due to interest rate parity, one must note that this is a phenomenon dependant on fixed exchange rates and inherent to the free market. Unlike capitalism, interest does not exist within the Islamic economic system and so aggregate demand is not dependant on monetary policy per se, rather fiscal policy is used by the state to stimulate the economy. Such an alternative is not a new discovery and was even used after the Great Depression, due to fixed exchange rates under the interwar gold standard.

II.   **Deflation**: One of the most important criticisms of the gold standard is that it is susceptible to deflation due to a lack of currency supply. This is often considered to be just as bad as inflation (if not worse). Deflation is essentially the antithesis of inflation, it is the persistent decrease in prices within an economy over a particular time period. The reduction of prices due to a lower money supply causes the currency to appreciate and in such an instance, economies may suffer from the following phenomena:

- The delayed consumption/expenditure effect occurs when households anticipate deflation, causing a lack of consumption due to a higher propensity to save. In other words, falling prices reflect a higher valued currency so consumers delay their consumption in order to benefit from buying the same quantity with less money (as goods and services become relatively cheaper).

- A deflationary climate often engenders a 'liquidity trap' which makes monetary policy ineffective (see appendix VII). When prices fall rapidly, nominal interest rates are often close or equal to zero and cannot be lowered any further by the central bank. At this point, extremely low opportunity costs for holding cash incentivises agents to hoard, thus stripping the central bank's ability to influence output via expansionary monetary policy.

- Borrowers have larger debt burdens due to an appreciation in currency value, this means that debtors would have to repay their debt with more than what was agreed upon before prices fell. This increase in debt burden leads to defaults and generally places heavy financial pressure on debtors, reducing the amount held in households, designated for spending and investment.

- Deflation has a strong impact in the labour market as firms lose out on profits due to a lack of sales. To cut costs they either fire employees and maintain the same wages or reduce wages and maintain disgruntled employees. Both provoke decline; for the former, higher unemployment is a precursor to lower growth. For the latter, lowering wages has an effect on disposable income, which could result in anaemic demand due to less spending. In addition to this, workers often resist nominal wages cuts, causing a rise in real wages and a fall in unemployment, which depresses the economy further.

However, upon inspection, some fears attached to this phenomenon can be immediately discarded, merely due to the framework of the Islamic economic system. Capitalist monetary policy is generally inefficacious under Islam due to a completely different currency and a strict prohibition of interest. So using these tools to solve the issues of deflation become irrelevant. Let us analyse the actual threats that could harm the Islamic economy.

To begin, the notion that a lower price level leads to real wage unemployment and consequently a spiral of decline, is not always theoretically justified. Mild deflation is generally considered innocuous if there is an efficient flow of the right information, such that the market is able to anticipate a reduction in prices and correct itself to reach an equilibrium with minimal lag. This could allow the economy to expand (or at the very least stabilise), even during a deflationary climate. Indeed this may be easily said on paper but the reality is, some variables take longer than others to adjust. The main worry and perhaps the reason why in theory, the labour market takes time to adjust for deflation, is better explained through the Keynesian sticky wage theory.[24] This is a phenomenon, in which wages remain constant or respond slower to a change in an economy's output. In this context, the reaction to falling prices within the labour market is subject to a time lag, primarily due to 'wage stickiness'.

---

[24] Keynes, 1936

In more methodical terms, economic agents negotiate labour contracts upon a fixed wage. During this period, if expected prices match the current price level then unemployment and output equilibrate but if expected prices rise, wages follow and vice versa. At times of deflation, Keynes suggested that workers would resist nominal pay cuts, as they fail to realise that prices have also deflated and so in 'real' ignorance they suffer from a 'money illusion'. The concern here is that a higher markup for firms and businesses would lead to a higher level of unemployment rather than wage stagnation, as the former is cost efficient and clears the market in the short run (albeit with harsh aggregate consequences), whilst the latter prolongs equilibration and could also lead to a higher level of unemployment.

In an Islamic economy, unemployment due to deflation would be rare, as wages are not sticky down and markets and contracts are generally less rigid and more flexible:

- Firstly, it is important to realise that at times of deflation prices are falling. Many seem to overlook at this point, that deflation would also mean lower production costs, which essentially allow firms and businesses to maintain a profit. It is for this reason that economies in history were able to grow at times of deflation, particularly with the help of technological advancement; as prices fell, so too did costs, which allowed for growth and prosperity.

- In terms of resilience, the Islamic ideology pumps key ideas through to society and builds a solid understanding of the economic reality, facilitating the computation of various concepts such as real versus nominal, long versus short term, et cetera. This is invaluable to overcome price rigidity. Capitalism's conflation between value and price has created a labour market, in which workers fail to realise that whilst nominal wages have changed, real wages have remained constant. Contrastingly, one would expect workers in an Islamic society to observe wages not through the nominal but in real terms (true worth in the market). Whilst the state should actively propagate indicators to demonstrate real wage consistency, this ideological understanding allows the labour market to reach an equilibrium faster, as workers are able to autonomously appreciate prices within the economy.

- There is also a general abhorrence towards reducing wages, due to the effects that accompany nominal rigidity, such as worker resignation, uproar and even sabotage. In most cases, this can result in unemployment (as firms face higher costs in maintaining constant wages). To combat these problems, Islam as an ideology maintains concepts such as *rizq* (provisions) which teaches the worker to be content with what has been bestowed upon him, *al-qadaa wal qadar* (the divine decree), which teaches the worker that there are matters beyond his control, *sabr* (patience), which teaches the worker to remain patient for nominal pay cuts are a short run necessity, et cetera. In this regard, Muslims would seldom become distraught by wage reduction, for it is within their proclivity to appreciate the aforementioned. Thus, the labour market in Islam is much more resilient to exogenous shocks. In fact, it is generally forbidden to rebel/strike against the employer after the employee has signed a contract. Rather the state acts as the primary modus operandi (providing the rights of a contract were violated) for the worker to resolve issues in a civil and structured manner. Firms and businesses would therefore be less fearful to reduce wages. This should not be mistaken as an opportunity for exploitation as this would be treated as an act of injustice.

To summarise this point; in order for any labour market to combat falling prices, a symmetric and efficient flow of the right information is indispensable. Furthermore, the economy should be set up to avoid market rigidity, so that correcting for the effects of deflation is a smooth process with minimal lag. Finally, the delayed consumption effect under Islam is less severe; as nominal wages fall, proper economic understanding and the correct Islamic concepts would suppress a downward shift in spending as it is understood that real wages are unchanged and that one should always seek to use his wealth within the economy as opposed to saving it. With a deterrent to save, and a lack of interest (which often acts as an incentive to hoard), the main avenue for a return would be through investment, thus stimulating the economy further. In addition to this, the state would have to do what is within its capacity to raise the disposable income of consumers so as to balance out the impact of wage cuts, providing they have fallen in real terms. Wealth re-injection would therefore be a key policy to counter a potential downturn.

Debt burdens on the other hand would not be such a large issue as the Islamic economy is not founded on debt nor an incessant incentive to borrow, in fact indebtedness is generally disliked and there is a strong incentive to clear any financial obligations in the short run, due to it being a matter accounted for in the hereafter. Defaults in an Islamic economy are therefore unlikely and also rare, primarily because the *Bait ul-Mal* actively attempts to assist those debtors who struggle to repay creditors, through the use of funds from the *zakah*.

III. **Scarcity**: There is also a concern for the global supply of gold. The claim being that there are not enough reserves to maintain such a currency, the effects of which are deconstructive and create an imbalance relative to an economy's transactions. One must look at this issue comparatively; this perception is undoubtedly built upon an understanding of the fiat currency which exists in supernormal amounts that certainly do not reflect the number of real transactions within the economy. Such a large quantity (primarily of credit), is mainly due to a belief that a larger supply of currency is akin to higher growth, when in reality this is a fallacy. In fact, the core effects are detrimental and most come in the form of inflationary pressure. Many claim that a higher money supply is necessary to eliminate the risk of insufficient transactions within an economy. So they have surmised that the gold standard would not work due to its limited quantity, meaning a lot of money must be invested in actually finding gold, mining and minting it, in order to increase its supply and keep up with growth.

Whilst the latter of this argument may be true, the former presumption upon which it is built (a lack of supply) is not entirely accurate. Gold is of course a commodity and any limitations faced in expanding its supply is much like any other commodity. In order for an economy to increase its money supply, it merely needs to purchase more gold or invest to find more of it. Furthermore, deflation as a result of a rise in the supply of goods and services relative to the supply of gold, ultimately reduces the costs for firms and businesses (as these too are prices), ultimately allowing them to continue production with a profit.

As for the fiat; growth on the back foot of harsh credit creation is deceptive and artificial when linked closely with the reality of recessions and mass inflation. In fact, an economy which contains excess currency is often unsustainable as the money supply is not reflective of the experienced economic growth, thus making it spurious. A currency limited in quantity and free from manipulation is not subject to this phenomenon as the supply is real and the effort required to attain it is linked to prices within the real economy. Indeed, the gold standard is the only currency that is sustainable in the long run as it substantiates the level of economic growth with real activity. In this respect, supporters of the fiat currency are in no position to criticise the limitations around supply.

IV.   **Maintenance**: Another inaccurate claim made against the gold standard is the cost of producing currency. Gold is supposedly an expensive commodity to maintain as one must invest in mining, extracting, minting, transporting, et cetera. Once again this point is relative; the costs of a fiat currency overpower the costs of maintaining a gold standard. Many also base this conjecture on an assumption that every individual must exchange gold and silver coins. However this does not have to be the case, the gold standard is also sustainable through paper backing, providing that it is fully backed and reflective of the gold reserves (specie) within the economy.

V. **Short-run price instability**: There are many arguments that suggest the gold standard is unstable in the short term due to high coefficient variation ratios over the gold epoch. However, as research has shown, the relative standard deviation is ineffective in measuring dispersion, when the mean of a data set is close to zero. In fact, contrary to popular belief, in much of the currency's history, average inflation per annum often remained low and stable (for example; from 1750 to 1850, inflation averaged roughly 2% over 50 years and even during the California gold rush, it averaged roughly 1.5% per year). A high CV/RSD is therefore an inaccurate indicator, when analysing the short-run price stability of a gold standard.

These are only some of the main arguments against the gold standard (although there are many others). It is clear however that the currency has much more to offer than the common myths of deflationary cycles, monetary rigidity, high costs, et cetera. The power in any medium of exchange is the manner in which it is used and the degree to which it integrates with the economy. It is therefore incumbent for the Islamic economy, to manage the gold standard appropriately, which would consequently maximise its impact on the economic system.

HISTORICAL GOLD PRICES:

Gold prices have historically remained relatively stable for a very long time. However, after the world detached themselves from their 'golden fetters', the price of Gold per troy ounce rose exponentially. The following data demonstrates the movement of gold prices (annual average) from 1850 to 2014:

*Prices are expressed in terms of the USD ($) to four SF.

1850: **18.93**	1890: **18.94**	1930: **20.65**	1970: **36.02**	2010: **1,225**
1851: **18.93**	1891: **18.96**	1931: **17.06**	1971: **40.62**	2011: **1,572**
1852: **18.93**	1892: **18.96**	1932: **20.69**	1972: **58.42**	2012: **1,669**
1853: **18.93**	1893: **18.96**	1933: **26.33**	1973: **97.39**	2013: **1,531**
1854: **18.93**	1894: **18.94**	1934: **34.69**	1974: **154.0**	2014: **1,264**
1855: **18.93**	1895: **18.93**	1935: **34.84**	1975: **160.9**	
1856: **18.93**	1896: **18.98**	1936: **34.87**	1976: **124.7**	
1857: **18.93**	1897: **18.98**	1937: **34.79**	1977: **147.8**	
1858: **18.93**	1898: **18.98**	1938: **34.85**	1978: **193.4**	
1859: **18.93**	1899: **18.94**	1939: **33.42**	1979: **306.0**	
1860: **18.93**	1900: **18.96**	1940: **33.85**	1980: **615.0**	
1861: **18.93**	1901: **18.98**	1941: **33.85**	1981: **460.0**	
1862: **18.93**	1902: **18.97**	1942: **33.85**	1982: **376.0**	
1863: **18.93**	1903: **18.95**	1943: **33.85**	1983: **424.0**	
1864: **18.93**	1904: **18.96**	1944: **33.85**	1984: **361.0**	
1865: **18.93**	1905: **18.92**	1945: **34.71**	1985: **317.0**	
1866: **18.93**	1906: **18.90**	1946: **34.71**	1986: **368.0**	
1867: **18.93**	1907: **18.94**	1947: **34.71**	1987: **447.0**	
1868: **18.93**	1908: **18.95**	1948: **34.71**	1988: **437.0**	
1869: **18.93**	1909: **18.96**	1949: **31.69**	1989: **381.0**	
1870: **18.93**	1910: **18.92**	1950: **34.72**	1990: **383.5**	
1871: **18.93**	1911: **18.92**	1951: **34.72**	1991: **362.1**	
1872: **18.94**	1912: **18.93**	1952: **34.60**	1992: **343.8**	
1873: **18.94**	1913: **18.92**	1953: **34.84**	1993: **359.8**	
1874: **18.94**	1914: **18.99**	1954: **35.04**	1994: **384.0**	
1875: **18.94**	1915: **18.99**	1955: **35.03**	1995: **383.8**	
1876: **18.94**	1916: **18.99**	1956: **34.99**	1996: **387.8**	
1877: **18.94**	1917: **18.99**	1957: **34.95**	1997: **331.0**	
1878: **18.94**	1918: **18.99**	1958: **35.10**	1998: **293.2**	
1879: **18.94**	1919: **19.95**	1959: **35.10**	1999: **279.0**	
1880: **18.94**	1920: **20.68**	1960: **35.27**	2000: **279.1**	
1881: **18.94**	1921: **20.58**	1961: **35.25**	2001: **271.0**	
1882: **18.94**	1922: **20.66**	1962: **35.23**	2002: **309.7**	
1883: **18.94**	1923: **21.31**	1963: **35.09**	2003: **363.4**	
1884: **18.94**	1924: **20.69**	1964: **35.10**	2004: **409.7**	
1885: **18.94**	1925: **20.64**	1965: **35.12**	2005: **444.7**	
1886: **18.94**	1926: **20.63**	1966: **35.10**	2006: **603.5**	
1887: **18.94**	1927: **20.64**	1967: **34.95**	2007: **695.4**	
1888: **18.94**	1928: **20.66**	1968: **39.31**	2008: **872.0**	
1889: **18.93**	1929: **20.63**	1969: **41.28**	2009: **972.4**	

The price of gold from 1850-2013. Prices from 1850-1994 were taken from Timothy Green's Historical Gold Price Table and converted from GPB to USD on 25/10/15. Prices from 1995-2008 were taken from Kitco.com, based on the LPM fix and prices from 2008-2014 were taken from Nma.org on 24/10/15.[25]

[25] NMA, 2015

VI. BUSINESS CYCLE THEORY

Synopsis: Various schools of thought can help us understand the nature of a business cycle and its causes, but it is Islam that ultimately provides a solution to this systemic issue.

According to the National Bureau of Economic Research (NBER), the United States conceived 33 business cycles from 1854 to 2009.[26] Each varied in severity and length, some lasted for months whilst others persisted for many years. The phases of a business cycle are generally understood and agreed upon between major economic schools of thought. However, most differ on what engenders a cycle and how economies transition from one phase to another. For the purpose of comprehension, the graph below illustrates a full business cycle and how real gross domestic product fluctuates over time:

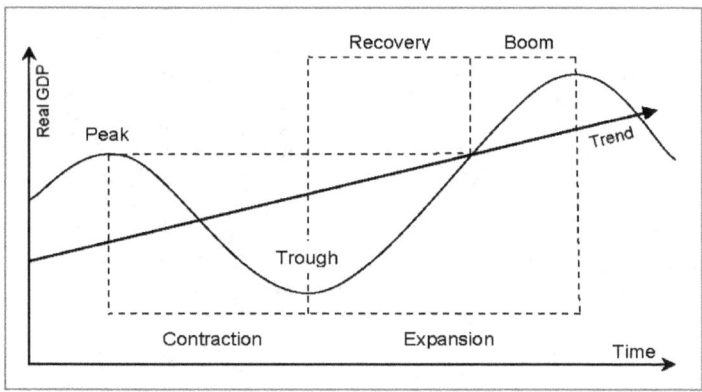

The business cycle has become an axiom within economic discourse and many have even deemed it to be ubiquitous within all markets. As we shall see, cyclical fluctuations are far from naturally occurring phenomena and should not be considered postulates, rather specific to capitalism and in particular certain traits that are ingrained within the ideology. Before we analyse various theories on this matter, it is important to understand the four stages of a business cycle.

PHASES OF THE CYCLE:

Boom/Peak: At this stage, the economy is sustaining a high level of aggregate demand, production is therefore at its peak and unemployment is low. Firms and businesses consequently benefit (in terms of profit) from the enhanced economic climate. Money is changing hands at a higher velocity and the economy is at a strong level of productivity, that is to say it is expanding in terms of real gross domestic product.

Recession/Contraction: Although the aforementioned 'boom' may seem prodigious, it is short-lived by its antithesis. In a recession, the economy is said to be shrinking in real terms. This means that demand is falling, due to less consumer expenditure and investment, which is kindled by a lack of confidence. Firms and businesses begin to make less profit due to lower levels of production and these costs are transferred onto the labour market causing unemployment to rise. Prices are falling and overall there is a decline in an economy's productivity, that is to say it is contracting.

Bust/Trough: This is the most depressed point in a business cycle. Here the economy is suffering from a prolonged period of anaemic gross domestic product, which essentially translates to low levels of aggregate demand, poor consumer spending and high levels of saving due to a lack of confidence in the economy. Likewise investment is low and the economy is at a poor level of productivity, that is to say it is stagnant.

Recovery/Expansion: At this point, the economy begins to expand once again. It is said to be growing in real terms as it faces a higher level of aggregate demand, which causes production to rise. Firms and businesses are enjoying larger profits, which pushes unemployment down. Prices begin to rise, money begins to change hands at a faster rate, as households begin to spend more whilst investors also become more confident. Overall, the economy gradually enhances its level of productivity (towards a boom), only to fall into the same cycle once again.

<u>KEYNESIAN THEORY</u>[27]:

In 1936, John Maynard Keynes theorised in his magnum opus 'The General Theory of Employment, Interest and Money', that contractionary phases within the business cycle were primarily due to changes in aggregate demand. According to his theory, in equilibrium total aggregate demand was equal to total spending within a closed economy and this demand consisted of consumption, investment and government expenditure. If planned aggregate demand fell due to a shock, then the resulting impact would create a recessionary gap. As a result, the economy must undergo economic adjustment in order to clear the effects of decline, so as to initiate a recovery.

By using the notion of an equipoise between planned and actual expenditure, Keynes described how during periods of lower production, wages would need to decrease as firms and businesses would shift higher costs onto the labour market in order to maintain the same level of output and profit. In an ideal world this would allow the market to reach an equilibrium, however after the Great Depression in 1929, economists realised that this took a much longer time to occur.

John Keynes famously explicated this issue by blaming the time lag on wages that were sticky down. As firms and businesses face higher costs, they do not wish to reduce wages due to the undesired impact within the labour market. Lower wages cause employees to feel undervalued and discriminated, leading to a lack of productivity and potential worker sabotage, ultimately reversing the desired effect. As a result of these complications, the labour market fails to clear when wages are reduced and so firms and businesses resort to firing workers; unemployment rises and revenue falls at an even greater rate.

To remedy this anaemic aggregate demand, Keynes shifted the neoclassical paradigm by suggesting a more interventionist approach, which was to increase government expenditure using expansionary fiscal policy. He was certainly antipathetic to the economic norm, as it allowed for markets to autonomously

                                                      Keynes, 1936; 1923 [27]

equilibrate over a lengthy and potentially dangerous period. In response to such a proclivity, he famously stated that "*In the long run we are all dead. Economists set themselves too easy, too useless a task, if in tempestuous seasons they can only tell us, that when the storm is long past, the ocean is flat again*".[27]

Keynes opined that fiscal stimulus worked as a core stabiliser to reduce the amplitude of a recession via the multiplier effect, ultimately accelerating the rate at which the economy reaches full employment. Such policy also facilitated the suppression of 'animal spirits', which was a term he coined to describe certain predilections held amongst society; particularly 'the paradox of thrift', where the propensity to save rises in a recession due to a lack of confidence, thus depressing the economy further.

In this respect, government expenditure (even if this involved deficit spending) could restore confidence and ameliorate aggregate demand; closing the recessionary gap and shifting the economy back to equilibrium - providing the positive effects of higher spending overrides the negative effects of higher interest rates (see appendix VIII). Keynes also suggested that monetary policy could be used to stimulate the economy, but was often inefficacious in a recession due to a 'liquidity trap' (whereby cash injections fail to regulate the interest rate) and so deficit spending would be the likely alternative.

MONETARIST THEORY[28]:

Milton Friedman was a key proponent of the monetarist school of thought. Monetarism describes a model in which the money supply is the basis for fluctuations in the business cycle. According to Friedman, a rapidly expanding money supply would give birth to volatile levels of inflation in the long run (see appendix IX) whereas a rapidly contracting supply would cause an economic downturn characterised by deflationary prices. This model also focuses on the flexibility of markets during a contractionary phases. Monetarists ultimately believe that to prevent such a phenomenon from occurring, economies must maintain a stable level of money supply.

---

[28] Friedman, 1987

Monetarists often blame the Great Depression on the actions of the Federal Reserve and the fact that they allowed the money supply to rapidly contract. In this respect, many have praised the school for being able to provide an insight into economic history. A good example of this is in 1979, when interest and inflation in the United States were very high and the Federal Reserve made the decision to reduce the money supply, so as to reduce prices. This resulted in a recession; characterised by sharp deflationary pressures and high levels of unemployment.

Like the Keynesian model, monetarism is more descriptive than prescriptive. In some cases, proponents have suggested that the money supply needs to be regulated and stabilised. This is somewhat general, amorphous and unhelpful as there are many classifications of money and monetarists have failed to define a particular area that must be controlled. Even then, regulating the money supply would be an extremely tedious job for the central bank, rendering such a proposition infeasible. Hitherto, it seems that both the Keynesian and Monetarist school of thought provide an excellent diagnosis of the business cycle but fail to impart a comprehensive cure for it altogether.

AUSTRIAN THEORY[29]:

Austrian economists Ludwig von Mises and Friedrich August von Hayek are becoming increasingly popular in contemporary economics. This is primarily due to their tendentious theory on business cycles, which maintains that expansionary monetary policy pushes investors to commit to 'malinvestments' that are destined to fail albeit without the knowledge of the investor.

In more methodical terms, due to the incessant capitalist growth imperative, economies tend to prefer an accelerated growth rate over a natural one, as the former brings future opulence into the present. To achieve this insatiable desire for growth, central banks begin to inject more credit into the economy. If interest is the price of money, a higher money supply ultimately lowers the interest rate and ultimately stimulates aggregate demand through investment due to lower borrowing costs.

Hayek, 1929; Mises, 1949 [29]

As a result of these extra funds in circulation, the economy begins to enter an unsustainable and accelerated expansionary phase. Due to a general fear of recession, economies that enter such an artificial boom prefer to decrease interest rates even further, so as to maintain an ostensible growth rate. This not only delays the contractionary phase (which equilibrates the economy), but it also exacerbates its impact (due to a further increase in malinvestment), raising the risk of a harsher crisis.

Mises refers to this phenomenon as 'overconsumption' in his book titled 'The Theory of Money and Credit'.[30] This is a situation in which agents overestimate the economic climate and as a result choose to consume more. However this overconsumption is based on credit that is not backed by real savings. Hayek even extrapolated this to the fractional-reserve system that gives out more loans than real savings.[31] As a result of this defective behaviour, many commit to long term investments in the short run that are destined to fail.

The sub-prime mortgage crisis is a good representation of the Austrian business cycle theory. This was essentially a period when the Federal Reserve implemented loose monetary policy and hence, interest rates were at an all-time low (fundamentally due to the dot-com bust). As a result, lower mortgages incentivised households in the US to borrow more than they could afford to pay back, under the illusion that low interest rates and easy credit would persist in the future. This is more commonly known as a housing bubble, where prices become distorted (overvalued) and do not reflect reality. This kindled an unsustainable level of economic activity and ultimately lead to the demise of many long term construction projects and mortgage decisions, which affirmed the Austrian model.

Many within this school are often considered to be heterodox economists, fundamentally due to their understanding of reality. Such a divide (between orthodoxy and heterodoxy) is made clear upon attempts to explicate the Great Depression. Whilst Keynesian economists claim that it was a product of rapidly contracting aggregate demand, Austrian economists blame the

---

[30] Mises, 1912
[31] Hayek, 1929

failure of monetary policy. In their eyes, the FED used expansionary monetary policy (by proliferating credit), inviting malinvestments that ultimately turned bad. If we look to history and various crises, one is certainly able to reconcile them with this theory, due to the many credit bubbles that have been conceived as a result of inefficient monetary policy.

Austrian economists generally believe that the market should be left to equilibrate and run its course. However, some have proposed preventative solutions such as a gold standard, whilst the majority have suggested stricter monetary policy (or abolishing the fractional reserve system), to prevent interest rates from declining to artificially low levels; inviting unsustainable malinvestments. Many critics believe that this theory assumes a level of naïvety amongst investors (especially in the contemporary world with more efficient markets), in that they are unable to sense the economy's health, so as to evade malinvestment. This is slightly ironic, given that Austrian economists interminably emphasise the virtues and credibility of the free market and its mechanisms.

ISLAM'S REMEDY:

To begin, it must be noted that each of the aforementioned theories maintain a unique focus. Keynesians believe that volatility in aggregate demand give birth to business cycles and to mitigate a recession, governments must use expansionary fiscal policy. Monetarists believe that sharp alterations in the money supply cause price instability and in managing this variable, one would suppress economic downturns. Austrians believe that an irresponsible banking sector coupled with failed monetary policy, are the main precursors to malinvestment and consequently a sharp decline in growth, thus to eradicate or restructure these issues, would be to act in a preventative measure against the booms and busts of the business cycle.

It seems that most theories on this matter, tend to prescribe acute (short-term) remedies to a chronic illness. Keynesian and Monetarist analysis seem to tacitly accept a ubiquitous business cycle in their attempts to tame the bust via monetary and fiscal policy. In the former school; a stimulus may reduce the severity of a downturn but it in no way prevents it from occurring in the future. Likewise in the latter; monetary regulation (in keeping the money supply stable) is not a remedy to long term fluctuations in growth. However, the Austrian theory seems to provide a more (albeit not totally) preventative approach, in that it attempts to resolve the business cycle itself as opposed to its effects. Even then, the support for a more free-market (by stripping away the governments monetary powers and the banking sectors management over the money supply) is far from a panacea, in fact it could even kindle the matter further.

Islam looks to the short run 'diagnosis' made by the Keynesian school of thought and provides an effective method of obviating real wage unemployment with a more effective value based system. As we have previously discussed, Islam values wages not through the lens of price rather through through their true worth to society, so individuals look through the real rather than constantly falling prey to the nominal. Additionally, the Islamic economy is also more resilient to shocks in aggregate demand due to key ideological concepts (such as *rizq* and *taqwa)* that filter through to society, which ultimately prevent problems such as worker sabotage, resignation, et cetera. In other words, the speed at which Islam reaches an equilibrium is much faster due to a lack of monetary rigidity and better expectations within the labour market.

The Islamic economic system also satiates concerns within the Monetarist and Austrian theory, with a remedy to monetary volatility through the bimetallic standard; preventing harsh inflationary/deflationary pressures. This would also thwart agents from manipulating the supply of currency in order to artificially push interest rates down, with the objective of stimulating the economy. In fact, the Islamic economy is immune to the artificial signals of interest as it eradicates the variable altogether. This ultimately eliminates malinvestments, suppresses overconsumption and puts an end to the perpetual capitalist predilection for unsustainable, transient growth.

Most economic downturns (of an endogenous nature) seem to emerge from the financial sector. As we shall see, with an entirely different model of finance, Islam deracinates the contemporary financial modus operandi and heavily restricts the possibility of endogenous shocks, protecting the economy from decline. The business cycle is an alien concept within the Islamic economic system and so there are no Islamic theories on this matter per se. This is not due to incomprehension nor incapacity but primarily because Islam has never had to deal with such a phenomenon. The only explanation to this, is that the Islamic system completely removes endogenous volatility, which is a significant point to consider as the business cycle is an inescapable assumption within all economic models.

Whilst Islam extirpates issues of an endogenous origin, this is not to say that exogenous shocks are a fictitious matter. Rather, they are primarily ephemeral as opposed to chronic and require smart monetary and or fiscal policy to mitigate. It seems then, that Keynesian theory is the best reference for interpreting the effects of a contractionary phase of an exogenous origin at the time of a downturn itself. As this book has demonstrated in the fifth chapter, the Islamic economic system is well equipped in dealing with such a threat of decline, and with the help of emergency funds, expansionary fiscal policy could remedy the economy of its recessionary malaise.

Finally, the core connective between all of the aforementioned theories is an unabating capitalist growth imperative, which incentivises a higher (insofar as it is unnatural) level of aggregate demand through monetary and fiscal policy. This proclivity for growth is often the underlying source of a boom/bust cycle and it is Islam that completely alters such a mentality. By focusing on distribution rather than growth, the Islamic economy does not need to stimulate aggregate demand and interfere with the natural rate of expansion. As a result, it averts the business cycle and its effect entirely. As we have consistently seen throughout this book, the ideological understanding ingrained within the Islamic economic system is the ultimate panacea to the maladies of capitalism.

VII. THE BANKING SECTOR

Synopsis: Banks with the freedom to exploit consumer savings and gamble risk based assets on financial markets for short term profits, push the economy into crises. The source of such autonomy lies with the laissez-faire system; liberal capitalism.

In the late 1930's, capitalism endured one of the most inimical financial crises ever known to man. The Great Depression, in modern history, is infamously known as the epitome of economic disintegration. During this crisis, worldwide gross domestic product fell by roughly 15%, unemployment reached an average of 25% and trade declined steeply by more than 50%.[32] The source of such economic horror stemmed from the financial sector; as a result of the stock market crash of 1929 and the rampant bank failures that ensued, financial institutions were the ones that ultimately plunged the global economy into a harsh depression that lasted for almost a decade.[33]

Ever since the Great Depression, governments around the world have worked assiduously to avert a similar catastrophe, even if it meant bailing out banks from dire situations like a credit crisis. This was evident when the UK nationalised Northern Rock and when the US orchestrated the purchase of Bear Stearns by JP Morgan Chase. However, these efforts died in vain when the investment bank 'Lehman Brothers' defaulted, causing a chain reaction on Wall Street and within the financial market, forcing governments to inject vast amounts of wealth into the banking sector in order to avoid economic free-fall.

These events are the most severe forms of financial crises and as history has shown, they are often triggered by endogenous shocks - the greatest source of which are financial institutions such as banks. Indeed, the banking system is considered to be a deadly poison within capitalism, a source of many issues and an initiator of crises that are beyond control. To understand the extent to which they affect the economy, we must understand the function of a bank within the financial sector.

---

[32] Szostak, 1995
[33] Clare, 2012

Firstly, we must acknowledge that economic agents within a laissez-faire system operate with high levels of autonomy to act as they please, usually in order to maximise profit. Adam smith writes extensively on how agents work for the optimum in society and that they should generally be left alone. This is to ensure that the free market stays distant from a command economy, leaving man to operate for the betterment of society. However, as we have seen, profit maximising agents that are generally deregulated, tend to corrupt the market's function of allocating resources between producers and consumers.

Some of these agents (such as governments and monetary authorities) are even in a position to set laws that others must abide by. This is an important point to remember as it will help us understand how the policy maker is connected to those who act out the policy. Indeed, it is amongst those who command the economy, where most issues originate. This is to say that the manner in which capitalism is constructed is its own flaw. At the heart of these fundamental sources of error lie the banks. These agents have a powerful influence on the money supply within a free market system, especially considering fiat is adopted as a base for currency, meaning that banks have more lucrative incentives and are not pegged by a fixed standard.

The banking system can be split into three core sections. The first is the retail or commercial banking sector, which deals with the monetary wealth of consumers and their deposits through basic loaning and borrowing mechanisms. The second is the investment banking sector, involving agents that perform various financial activities such as market making, proprietary or client based trading and providing advice or assistance on merges and acquisitions. The third are known formally as central banks and are entities that play a pivotal role in policy making within the capitalist framework. However, their primary function is to manage the supply of an economy's currency and so they behave as a monopolist in this regard. This is a rough overview of the banking system, let us now investigate and scrutinise each component, so as to understand their role within capitalism's financial sector.

The industrialist Henry Ford once aptly said: "*It is well enough that people of the nation do not understand our banking and monetary system for if they did, I believe there would be a revolution before tomorrow morning.*"[34]

Banking as a process has been heavily misconceived by many due to outdated economic teaching. The main issue with such an understanding is that it is dipped in classical theory and regurgitated by teachers and lecturers with little substance. Students of economics have failed to realise that this model of banking does not reflect reality. To make matters worse, most politicians and economists who have developed their understanding based merely on what has been taught to them also work around this model to organise the economy.

Whilst it is well established that individuals generally put aside their surplus wealth by placing it in a savings account (to gain a return through interest), some believe that these deposits remain stagnant for a 'rainy day'. In actuality, banks inherit and abuse these deposits to chase interest based profit. A large portion of society have also understood banks to be middle men or what economists call 'financial intermediaries'. Although ubiquitous, this understanding is also not entirely accurate, for it is built upon an assumption that banks take wealth from savers in the form of deposits and loan them out to borrowers who are able to then fund their businesses; in this cycle, household savings reflect financial investment.

By charging borrowers a higher interest rate than what is promised to savers, banks are able to receive a profit for their financial service. However, this suggests that banks are limited by borrowers and savers from reckless lending and massive profits. However, in reality banks have the ability to manipulate the amount of money they hold through creating credit rather than depending purely on deposits. Before we explore the contemporary model, we must understand the orthodox view, so as to appreciate the variance between them.

---

[34] Ford, 1922

CONVENTIONAL RETAIL MODEL:

In the free market, households place their wealth into bank accounts for three core reasons; to avoid inflationary tax, to refrain from maintaining wealth in bulk and to profit from saving. Financial intermediaries have a strong proclivity to capitalise on this disposition to save by using consumer deposits for profit driven objectives. The philosophy being that there exists an abundance of impotent wealth within consumer accounts, that could potentially be used for more interest based loaning (entailing a greater profit for the bank). The main danger associated with such a system of borrowing/lending is a banking crisis. This is essentially the culmination of many issues that occur when elite banks (whose sole purpose is to maximise profit) control the flow of monetary wealth.

As mentioned, retail banks believe that the aggregate amount of money that consumers deposit sit idle in their accounts, when in reality they have the potential to generate more money and consequently more profit. As a result of this mentality, banks loan these funds out based on an assumption that depositors will not withdraw all of their wealth in the short run. There is a wider issue to this process but we will cover it in the next subtopic. Furthermore, monetary policy set by the central bank prevents a retail bank from loaning out 100% of consumer deposits by setting a reserve ratio/rate. For example, if the central bank sets a reserve rate of 5%, retail banks can loan back to the public only 95% of consumer deposits.

The surplus between what is loaned and returned is a profit for the bank; it being paid back is a process which bankers deem inevitable. The theory being that consumers will spend/invest these loans, which will ultimately go into the hands of an agent who has a propensity to save. This money is then re-injected back into the banking sector only to be loaned out once again for more interest based profit. Banks perpetuate this cyclical process until they accrue supernormal wealth, as a result of what is conventionally known as the 'money multiplier effect'.

Indeed, there is a high risk of using short term deposits for long term loaning as people may wish to withdraw their money at the end of the short run. When this occurs, banks may not be able to pay the consumer, for their savings do not actually exist within their account, or in other words, the banks have insufficient liquidity to make available these funds. In many cases this can cause tensions amongst the public. In fact, any indication of a deteriorating economic climate, can trigger societal panic as it kindles the idea of a potential loss in savings and thus a need to hedge one's losses through withdrawal.

Such trepidation could be triggered by a number of factors. In fact, a common example used to demonstrate the fragility of a fractional reserve system, is when the Central Bank issues a guarantee to consumers over their deposits. In this case, the collateral itself frightens savers, causing them to believe they may lose money due to some undisclosed problem with their respective bank. So whilst the policy initially intended to quell fear, it induced it! Such is the fragile nature of a house of cards. As a result of this anxiety, consumers rush to retail banks in order to withdraw their savings. This is what is known as a 'bank run', where consumers literally run to the banks to withdraw that which they may be unable to in the future. However, when people rush to withdraw in such a climate, they often find that banks are unable to return their hard earned savings and most are left with absolutely nothing.

Whilst this may sound shocking, it has been a common trend in history and even occurred during the financial crisis of 2008, where a lack of confidence in the economy incentivised mass withdrawals, instigating a crisis of illiquidity. Evidently then, financial institutions under a capitalist free market system retain maximum autonomy to make a profit at the expense of the people through the abuse of their wealth. Such activity within the banking sector has created many knock-on problems in the economy and has often led to capitulation. In fact, in the 19th and 20th century, most financial crises were linked to bank panics which then later morphed into recessions.

<u>CONTEMPORARY RETAIL MODEL:</u>

The aforementioned model is commonly used to represent the current banking system. Aside from the general theory that describes basic mechanism of a fractional reserve system, this banking model is built upon two ostensible assumptions:

I. **Passive banking:** The conventional model assumes that banks require the deposits of savers to begin loaning and initiate the money multiplier effect. In other words, banks are thought to be subject to the will of savers by their deposits. Indeed, it is true that savers are the agents that supply their deposits to banks and that banks are the agents whom use these deposits to generate interest based profit by loaning them out once again (given that a certain amount is retained), but this passivity and patience is not entirely accurate. In fact, banks do not require deposits to begin loaning funds, rather it is well known that they are able to create credit at no cost and loan these funds out in the form of debt (with interest) to borrowers.

II. **Monetary base:** The conventional model also assumes that the central bank has total control over the money supply, merely by adjusting the reserve ratio (the % of customer deposits retained before re-loaning) or by using expansionary/contractionary monetary policy to feed/ retract credit directly into and or out of the monetary base.

As for the former, economists believe that the reserve ratio effectively influences the money supply and restricts it from expanding capriciously. However, whilst this may be the theory, many economies currently sustain low reserve ratios or none at all and seldom do they use the indicator (determined by the demand and supply of credit). This has led to large and increasingly unsustainable levels of credit. In fact, according to The BoE, 97% of the UK's money supply has been generated in this manner.[35] Thus, banks adjust their base as they please and on their assessment of the economic climate, not purely on the reserve ratio.

McLeay, Radia and Thomas, 2014 [35]

As for the latter, expansionary monetary policy is utterly useless if what credit is created does not filter to the private sector. Evidently then, monetary authorities like the central bank are unable to influence the money supply through their policy given that the banking sector has been anaemic post financial crisis; as such, it is becoming increasingly difficult to maintain the vast reserves that are either being hoarded and or expanded by the banking system.

The main question we must ask is; do banks really loan out the funds of savers or is there another mechanism that generates large sums of profit and if so, how does this have an impact on the monetary base of an economy, given that banks are not passive. In reality, banks have the ability to create money from thin air and debit accounts with unsubstantiated funds. On this matter, the Bank of England states that "when banks make loans they create additional deposits for those that have borrowed the money" and "in the modern economy those bank deposits are mostly created by retail banks themselves."[36]

Take the fractional reserve system as an example. Saver A places £100 in his savings account, 90% of these funds are then loaned to borrower B whilst 10% are kept as reserves. Borrower B then re-injects his £90 into the bank and the same process continues until the supply of money is exhausted. If we were to compute this calculation, the amount of money in circulation (M_1) would amount to approximately £1000. One may ask at this point; how could £100 manifest into £1000? The answer to such a question comes down to the scope of money, which can be categorised into the following:

M0: This is the measure of notes and coins that circulate the economy. It includes bank reserves (often called the monetary base) and is roughly around 3% of M4. It is the narrowest definition for monetary supply and thus the most liquid.

M1: This is the measure of M0 in addition to cheques but excluding bank reserves. It is a large faction of the total money in circulation. M1 is less liquid than M0.

---

[36] Mankiw and Taylor, 2014

M2: This is essentially the measure of M1 but it also includes savings and money market accounts. M2 is putatively the main measure for credit within the economy. It is less liquid than M1.

M3: This includes M2, in addition to large and long term deposits. Unsurprisingly, this value is not available (it is very difficult to measure) due to its sheer size and magnitude. M3 is also less liquid than M2, with a wider and broader scope.

M4: This includes all funds within the money market, which is akin to the total money supply within the economy. M4 has the widest scope with the highest value and is astronomically larger than M0. The Graph on page 70, demonstrates the fluctuation of broad money from 1870 to 2010, with a brief explanation.

As we can see, there are various definitions for an economy's money supply. The elemental issue with the fiat currency is that it has given the financial sector the ability to develop various measurements that categorise the amount of money existent within the economy. In reality, the most meaningful values are derived from M0 and M4, together they demonstrate a growing disparity between real and superficial capital.

In order to understand how these definitions fit inside the current banking system, let us consider a historical example from the 16th century.[37] During this time, goldsmiths used to store precious metals and items in vaults to protect their wealth. Merchants noticed this and began to leave their gold coins with these goldsmiths for the same purpose. In return, they were handed receipts (bonds) that were essentially certificates of indebtedness. These bonds ultimately linked back to the one who stored the gold and so individuals could merely revisit the goldsmith to reclaim their money in due time.

This later developed into a mechanism whereby bonds were used as legal tender (currency) to pay for goods and services due to the value they held in the goldsmiths vault, as opposed to going to the bearer, withdrawing the money only to spend it again. By passing on issued paper, one would ultimately be

BoE, 2015 [37]

passing on the duty for the bearer to simply visit the goldsmith and reclaim what was left in gold by the original depositor. After realising this phenomenon, goldsmiths began lending out unsubstantiated bonds with interest, to make a large profit.

They did however retain the minimum amount based on the demand for withdrawals, so as to prevent the people from discovering they did not actually have the relevant funds in their account. By perpetuating this process goldsmiths became excessively rich and it was this system of finance that inevitably led to the current banking system and an aggregate rise in the money supply. Therefore, whenever the monetary base expands, it is indicative of credit proliferation. However, unlike this analogy, these funds are not real insofar as they are not backed by any tangible commodity, which only became a reality the world abandoned the gold standard.

The aforementioned capitalist system of banking, has now developed into a very different mechanism albeit based on the same fundamental principles. As we have seen, banks do not have the patience to wait for savers to deposit funds in order to give out loans. Instead, they create unsubstantiated funds by typing a few digits on a screen and deposit debt in the form of electronic funds into consumer accounts. Indeed, most money circulating the economy (M1) is generated in this way, much like the unsubstantiated bonds that were handed out and circulated by the goldsmiths. This also means that if debt (in the form of money) was repaid, the money supply would diminish completely, as society would be repaying what is due to the banks. This is the epitome of a debt driven system as it essentially means that capitalism must sustain debt if its economy is to have the relevant funds to survive.

Finally, it is important to note the fluctuation in M4, which is a core aggregate indicator of the money supply within the United Kingdom. When gross domestic product expands and contracts in short spaces of time, M4 (and other variables like it) is subject to a great deal of pressure as the overall level of credit changes rapidly in response to the financial climate.

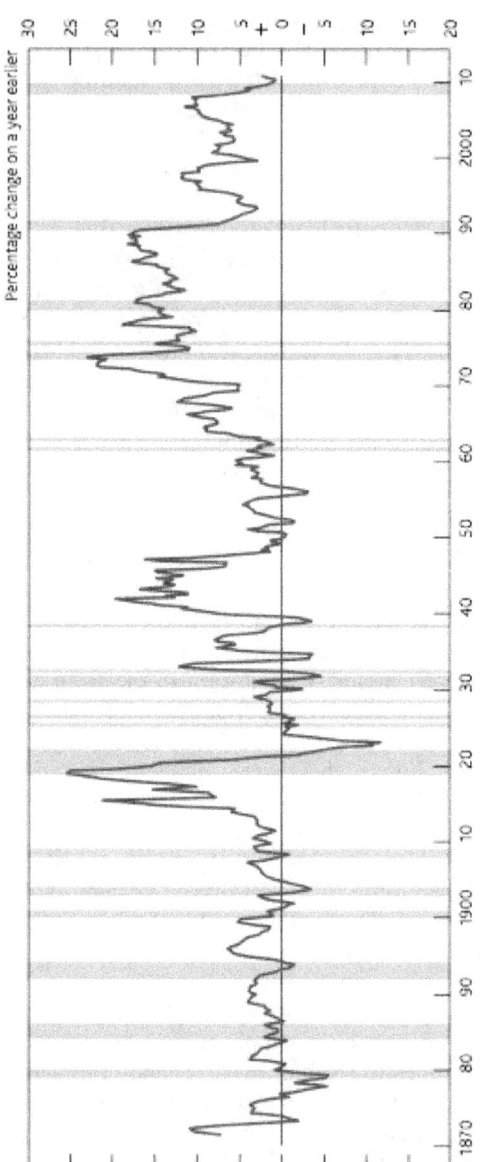

Sources: Bank of England, Capie, Webber (1985), Hills et al (2010).[38] The graph above illustrates the percentage change in M4 (y-axis) over approximately 150 years (x-axis). Recessionary periods are highlighted in grey. Annual recessions are graphed prior to 1924. Post 1924, two consecutive quarters of negative growth are shown. M4 is the widest scope/definition of money and accounts for the total money supply. It is often considered a useful indicator to understand the overall health of credit within the economy and is often affected by gross domestic product. Post 2010, M4 has remained relatively anaemic and has only been kept stable at this level due to popular quantitative easing programs.

Pettinger, 2014 [38]

INVESTMENT BANKING SECTOR:

Agents within this sector (investment bankers), are involved in the act of raising funds from their involvement in linking together investors/lenders and borrowers. They deal with governments from various countries, corporations of different sizes and even individuals from multifarious wealth brackets.

Their activity, although broad and general, can be split into the following sections within the financial market:

I.   **Client based trading:** This is where banks are able to trade on behalf of clients and profit from their service or from the gain that is made on each trade. In this process, the risk lies with the buyer of the financial asset and not the intermediary such as the investment bank.

II. **Proprietary trading:** This is where banks essentially bet on large financial assets for a direct gain as opposed to a commission from linking trades between clients. Wagers are generally high in risk as they depend on an assumption that either the financial asset will appreciate some time in the future or that the market will change in its favour. Alternatively, the antithesis can occur and the investment bank can lose a large amount of money.

III. **Market making:** This is where investment bankers create markets for buyers and sellers to come together with the objective of exchanging financial products. This facilitates the ability for buyers to locate sellers and vice versa. Investment banks therefore act as an intermediary and gain a profit for their service of creating a market.

IV. **Advising (mergers and acquisitions):** This is where investment banks assist agents such as companies in their decision to merge/acquire other companies. This assistance mainly comes in the form of advice, so as to ease the transition period. Banks essentially make a profit based on the size of the deal being made. The larger the merge or acquisition, the higher the profit. Investment bankers are also able to assist agents in raising funds on financial markets by selling financial products. In this case, profit is taken as a percentage of the yield. Investment banks can also advise/assist agents by issuing structured products (such as a combination of financial products) and or by underwriting (issuing liabilities or insurance).

Whilst each of the aforementioned activities paint a relatively innocuous image of investment banks, many economists have equated them to gamblers in a 'casino market', primarily based on the sheer uncertainty in proprietary trading, which forms the main and most lucrative activity in investment banking. Such precariousness has forced most banks to establish risk management sectors so as to analyse factors like credit, market trends and the credibility of assets as it is very common for assets to be falsely sold or evaluated. However, the negative sentiment is certainly true; these banks are infamous for being recognised as a deep rooted issue within the capitalist banking system, as a group of economic elite who have the ability to enter markets in order to make a massive profit from buying, selling and gambling risk heavy financial assets.

Although investment banks do not function in the same manner as retail bank (by lending/receiving deposits), they are widely known to associate with traditional retail banks for their own interests. JP Morgan, Merrill Lynch and the Salomon Brothers are all examples of institutions that quickly escalated in the investment banking sector after merging with retail banks.[39] It is also possible for financial institutions to engage in the retail and investment sector simultaneously. By doing this, investment bankers can dip their hands into large reserves of consumer based financial goods purely to gamble them on the financial market for risky profits.

One must not forget, this is the wealth of real people with very real problems. In fact, this became such a big issue that the US government maintained a transient policy that separated investment from retail banks with the intent to avoid a further

Knight, 2010 [39]

crisis after the Great Depression. The Glass-Steagall Act of 1933 meant that by law, banks could not collude, although this was later repelled by the Gramm-Leach-Bliley Act or the Financial Services Modernisation act of 1999.[40] Such is the nature of a failed economy, in that it cannot permanently enforce policies that prevent the misusage of wealth.

As a result of this gambling mentality, investment banks like Goldman Sachs can get away with pushing risks on to clients in exchange for millions whilst others like the Lehman Brothers capitulate from leverage based trade. Evidently, capitalism has given power to agents that are currently driving the real economy into financial chaos. To make matters worse, the orchestrators of such anarchy are well known to receive massive paycheques and bonuses for their financial duties! Furthermore, when the gambler loses, whether that be due to risk based proprietary trading or even exogenous shocks, they must be bailed out in order to prevent the whole economy from collapsing (examples: Northern Rock, Lloyd and Bear Stearns). In fact, on this matter alone, the UK has spent approximately £1.162 trillion in government funds (a large proportion of which originated from the taxpayer)[41] to bailout financial institutions, recuperate toxic assets and fix the financial sector from a climate of utter pandemonium left behind by the banks, which crippled the real economy for many years.

THE ROLE OF CENTRAL BANKS:

As a result of loose monetary activity and the collapse of many financial institutions during economic downturns, capitalism required a set of unified institutions to manage the fiat (in light of a switch from the gold standard). This necessity gave birth to central banks like the European Central Bank (ECB), the Bank of England (BoE) and the Federal Reserve (FED). These are essentially semi-autonomous entities with the primary function of managing the money supply within an economy through monetary policy such as controlling interest rates, adjusting the reserve rate and conducting open market operations.

---

[40] Rickards, 2012
[41] Rogers, 2013

Some have welcomed these institutions, as they are supposedly a tool to attain structural stability whilst others have scorned their existence. In fact, since their inception, central banks have often been blamed for their inability to prevent crises and have even been accused of ineffective policy by notable economists. Unlike retail and investment banks, these institutions are policy makers as opposed to policy takers. In this way they have monopolised the banking sector by their ability to set policies that others must abide. This book will dedicate a separate chapter in order to scrutinise monetary policy, so as to further understand the role that central banks play within the economy.

ISLAM'S ALTERNATIVE TO BANKING:

Firstly, the Islamic economic system removes any concept of a fractional reserve system to ensure that banks are not left to abuse deposits for profit driven purposes, affecting the health and condition of the economy. In response to this, economists often argue that banks are an instrumental part to any economy as they provide a service where people can store their hard earned wealth, and to strip them of such a fundamental, renders them useless. However, Islam has no sympathy for a corrupted banking sector, regardless of its elemental nature and will abolish it immediately, purging the economy of a severe illness.

In contrast to this perpetual tendency to save, the Islamic model directs economic agents towards re-injection through key ideological concepts. Whilst the free market system has an incentive for households to save money in the bank so as to gain interest, Islam maintains a disincentive to hoard through an enforced annual tax on surplus wealth and an incentive to spend via the potential reward from Allah (ﷻ).

As for the former the Almighty says: "*And let not those who hoard up that which Allah hath bestowed upon them of His bounty think that it is better for them. Rather, it is worse for them. That which they hoard will be their collar on the Day of Resurrection. Allah's is the heritage of the heavens and the earth, and Allah is Informed of what you do.*"[42]

Quran, 3:180 [42]

As for the latter, Allah's apostle said: *"O son of Adam, it is better for you if you spend your surplus (wealth), but if you withhold it, it is evil for you. There is (however) no reproach for you (if you withhold means necessary) for a living. And begin (charity) with your dependants; and the upper hand is better than the lower hand."*[43]

This is certainly an excellent usage of wealth, as it ultimately leads to an increase in economic distribution and productivity. In methodical terms, higher monetary injections allow for more money to change hands at a higher velocity and range, thus the economy enjoys improved equity and growth. This is a phenomenon that even the capitalists desire, although it seldom transpires within the free market. This is because banks offer a lucrative incentive (in the form of returns via interest on saving accounts) for households to hoard their wealth.

It should be clear that the elemental function of a bank is to store household wealth and it is Islam that restricts a bank's function to exactly this. If retail banks wish to profit within this sector, they will fail miserably as hoarding is categorically forbidden and whilst loaning is possible, banks receive exactly what is lent out and nothing on top of the principal.

Allah (ﷻ) says: *"O you who have believed, fear Allah and give up what remains [due to you] of interest, if you should be believers. And if you do not, then be informed of a war [against you] from Allah and His Messenger. But if you repent, you may have your principal - [thus] you do no wrong, nor are you wronged."*[44]

One must also note that retail banks are often dangerous during an economic downturn, as they give timorous households the ability to save their wealth as opposed to spending it. As a result of a reduction in consumption, the economy suffers from what John Maynard Keynes theorised as a 'paradox of thrift', where the propensity to save increases and aggregate demand falls, damaging the economy further.

---

[43] Ibn al-Hajjaj, ND
[44] Quran, 2:288-289

To combat such a scenario, Islam promotes spending and consequently enjoys a healthy expansion to counteract any ongoing contraction. This is one of many factors that can heal an economy in the short run, as it is a variable (expenditure) that feeds directly into aggregate demand. In other words, Islam contends the paradox of thrift with an alternative to saving through key Islamic concepts, which encourages households to shift their behaviour in favour of the economy.

Another issue with the fractional reserve system is that money is advanced to individuals over their collateral. This effectively traps wealth amongst those who have good credit ratings, which is often common in a higher social class. Islam sustains a direct system of profit and loss sharing projects that do not depend on credit level per se. Unlike capitalism, Islam advances money not to the rich (due to their collateral) but to individuals alike based on their projects. This reduces inequality as profits are distributed amongst all social classes as opposed to the wealthy and powerful.

Furthermore, credit creation under the current fractional reserve system is certainly an unjust act, as banks have the ability to create funds with absolutely no effort and gain profit from interest based loans, that is to say by charging the interest to society. In fact, if one wished to perform such an act, it would be recorded as a criminal offence. Indeed, blatant hypocrisy like this exists ubiquitously within capitalism. By allowing banks to commit such fraud, society essentially opens the gate to high levels of patronage over governments, corporations and individuals. This is to say; those who are able to control an economy's currency, also wield a high level of political power.

Islam strips this institutionalised fraud in its entirety by handing all monetary power to the state, rather than autonomous profit seeking, private entities. In addition to this, Islam establishes a gold standard, which further secures an economy's currency as it ensures that any money added to the monetary base is backed by effort (mining, transport, et cetera) as opposed to cheap credit manufactured at the touch of a single button.

As for investment banks that lurk within the financial sector; Islam suppresses any gambling mentality held within the minds of bankers, who take large sums of wealth and act on speculation, hoping to make a large financial gain. There is no environment (due to regulation and definitive contract based interaction) where any risk infested casino market can manifest:

The Almighty Allah (ﷻ) says in the Quran: *"They ask thee concerning wine and gambling. Say: "In them is great sin, and some profit, for men; but the sin is greater than the profit." They ask thee how much they are to spend; Say: "What is beyond your needs." Thus doth Allah Make clear to you His Signs: In order that ye may consider."*[45]

Rather what Islam does encourage, as an alternative to consumers and firms associating themselves with investment banks for investment based projects, is equity based partnerships on a profit and loss sharing basis where the risk is collectively spread between both agents. This form of finance will be discussed at length within the next chapter. Moreover, Islam does not subsidise the negative externality through banker bonuses or bailouts via taxpayer dominated funds (incentivising corruption), as this is an overt act of hypocrisy and a major injustice to the people.

So to conclude by summary; Islam opines wealth re-injection through spending and if consumers still wish to save, redistributive taxes are imposed on the annual amount of surplus wealth to incentivise higher expenditure. This facilitates wealth circulation, which increases the velocity at which money changes hands and who it changes between.

Islam strips away the current financial mechanism and replaces it with a sustainable equity based partnership system where profits and losses are shared by both parties. This removes the fabricated need for an investment bank to conduct all financial activity. Although these 'middle men' can exist to initiate links between economic agents for investment based projects, they are only rewarded for their service and contracts are only

---

[45] Quran, 2:219

concluded between the partners involved. Through such a system, individuals have more access to business related opportunities rather than constantly turning to the banks for interest based loans to fund or begin a project.

Islam hands monetary authority to the state and constructs the *Bait ul-Mal,* which acts as a public bank that is managed and regulated by the Caliph and his cabinet. More importantly, the removal of the fiat system and the establishment of a gold standard, withdraws the ability for any agent to continuously create money for nothing and charge the interest to society.

The Islamic economic system dismantles any form of capitalist oriented investment bank so as to protect the real economy from decline. However, some elemental functions such as market making and assisting investment prospects are not inherently problematic functions per se, in fact, they have often been practiced by the Muslims long before capitalism developed its financial modus operandi. It is therefore likely that the Islamic economy will optimise certain mechanisms, that do not inherently contradict the Islamic doctrine (*aqeedah*), to meet the criteria of the Islamic legal code (*sharia*). Aside from these minutiae, Islam radically alters the complex financial sector in which all of the aforementioned corruption occurs. This is primarily achieved through detailed contract based interaction, conditioned upon a mechanism of acceptance and offer, as we will later see in the following chapters.

Finally, the endemic gambling behaviour exhibited by most banks within capitalism, is categorically forbidden. More importantly, Islam prevents any agent from trapping large sums of real money in the financial market as opposed to investing it in the real economy, pushing growth and prices up but leaving real output behind. On an aggregate level, Islam's outlook towards the banking sector will surely attain structural stability and secure the economy from endogenous volatility.

VIII. MONETARY POLICY

Synopsis: Central banks employ monetary policy to unnaturally regulate the money supply. Capitalism's problems are systemic and cannot be resolved through pecuniary adjustments.

Monetary policy is generally set and altered by a central bank. These are powerful, semi-autonomous entities that regulate key economic indicators such as the consumer price index, interest rates, et cetera. To influence these variables, the central bank must regulate the economy's money supply, as it has a short run impact on economic activity and the rate of inflation, which is perhaps the biggest concern for policy makers.

However, economists have often been sceptical over a central banks ability to manage the economy. For example, when growth fell during the crisis, central banks failed to stimulate aggregate demand with loose monetary policy. To make matters even worse, many banks injected trillions into the financial sector under a monetary experiment, known as 'quantitative easing'. However, this manufactured credit failed to permeate and eventually became trapped due to a lack of confidence.[46]

As a result, the real economy suffered from depression for an even longer duration and one could argue that policy makers dug themselves deeper into the very hole they themselves created. In fact, the current global economy is still suffering from the harsh effects of the 2008 financial crisis and monetary policy remains a relatively inefficacious tool to improve the anaemic growth and aggregate demand.

Before we dwell into this subject, it is important to note that central banks currently use the following tools/policies to regulate the economy and its money supply:

I. $\uparrow/\downarrow$ the base rate to $\downarrow/\uparrow$ the money supply.
II. Sell/buy bonds in OMO's to $\downarrow/\uparrow$ the money supply.
III. Conduct quantitative easing to $\uparrow$ the money supply.
IV. $\uparrow/\downarrow$ the reserve requirement to $\downarrow/\uparrow$ the money supply.

---

[46] Positive Money, 2012

Interest is essentially the price of money or the cost of borrowing. In capitalism, such a concept is ubiquitous, as it is profit for the lender and thus a tool to regulate credit in the economy. Much like price, the interest rate influences the demand and supply for credit. The higher the interest rate, the more people are deterred from borrowing and vice versa. Indeed, if a monopolist is capable of manipulating the price mechanism, then monetary policy makers like the Bank of England and the Federal Reserve are akin to monopolists over credit, simply due to their ability to influence the interest rate.

When capitalism experienced the frequent busts of the business cycle, central banks quickly realised a method to tame the economy; by adjusting interbank lending rates they were able to control the flow of credit. These interest rates (such as the Federal Funds rate or the Euro Overnight Index Average) are attached to short-term collateralised loans, offered by central banks to retail banks at times of need. To manage the supply of money, central banks alter the level of interest; the higher the rate, the more it costs to borrow and vice versa. At times of deflation, central banks lower the rate to encourage banks to borrow more overnight. A cheaper rate incentivises lending, raising the money supply, aggregate demand and prices. Contrastingly, it can increase this rate to induce the antithesis, thus forcing banks to either increase their reserves so as to avoid borrowing or pass the costs on to their interest rates, ultimately lowering the money supply within the economy.

Interest is an axiom under the free market and it is perhaps the cornerstone of the contemporary global economy. However, there are many negative characteristics attached to the concept and its application. For example; interest raise the cost burden for debtors as it an extra amount on top of their loan. If the borrower fails to maintain repayments, interest will gradually accrue even more debt over the principal, which increases the probability of default. Investors also suffer from constant uncertainty in expected return, this is primarily because interest rates are often set according to the economic climate and are therefore volatile. To prevent a loss from such fluctuation, both investors and traders often speculate over interest rates and the price level, which subsequently leads to risk based trading.

Furthermore, in the current banking system, agents make deposits for nothing in return whilst retail banks charge high rates of interest to society. This imbalance in the flow of credit kindles inequality as money is constantly syphoned out of the real economy. It is also an incentive to continue loaning due to the profit involved. More loans reflect a higher level of credit creation (by virtue of the fractional reserve system), which inevitably induces inflation in the long run. To make matters worse, Economists often mistake the future return on this debt as an improvement in productivity, when in reality, profits gained by creditors are not backed by any real output.

In addition to this, there exists a perpetual battle to ensure interest rates are in line with inflation so as to control the supply of money and growth. As we know, lower interest rates can stimulate growth in the short run, but induce inflation in the long, pulling back output to its natural rate. Central banks hike rates to prevent inflation from rising above 2% (a level believed to attain maximum employment). If they are too slow or fast, price changes could be detrimental to GDP as interest may act as a deterrent when an incentive is needed and vice versa.[47]

Moreover, interest rates set by the central bank have a large influence on the propensity to save. A higher rate forces many to save more due to a higher rate of return on bonds as opposed to holding or borrowing cash for investment. As such, investors have an incentive to keep their capital in banks as opposed to using it to stimulate growth through projects. This is a major hindrance as it can disturb the natural tendencies of an agent in respect to his consumption and savings decisions. Interest also distorts the behaviour of households, as they discount the future due to the expected effects on consumption in the present. In other words, there is a constant inclination within society to combat the future by accelerating economic activity in the

---

[47] ONS, 2014

present. This skews short term consumption and production behaviour, causing negative externalities for the future. These are some of the core problems that are generally associated with interest. Many often insist that it is a useful tool to influence the economy, however given the aforementioned effects it is clear that interest is an ill that requires treatment.

QUANTITATIVE EASING:

In the early stages of the financial crisis, central banks slashed interest rates to counter a steep decline in aggregate demand. However, the downturn was so severe that lowering interest rates (close to zero) failed to achieve this. Furthermore, banks stopped lending altogether due to a worry that their existing loans would not be repaid. When monetary policy had been exhausted, many turned to another method of stimulating growth, known formally as 'quantitative easing' or QE. This essentially involved credit creation by the central bank, to purchase financial securities (particularly bonds). Fresh money would fill the cash reserves of retail banks, allowing them to make more loans, which would ultimately stimulate aggregate demand and growth. Now however, central banks use quantitative easing as an active policy to maintain the economy, in fact the ECB recently launched its massive QE program to boost cash reserves from €13 billion to an egregious €60 billion, whilst the FED have amassed (through quantitative easing) more than $4 trillion![48] Although this may seem like an effective way of pumping up the economy, there are certain problems that are affiliated with quantitative easing.

Firstly, increasing the supply of money has deteriorated the value of the fiat extensively. Secondly, by injecting large amounts of credit into the financial sector, banks are more prone to moral hazard. Thirdly, quantitative easing is not a method to solve a crisis, rather it is a means to delay its end. It does not fix the business cycle, but moves the brunt of the bust to a later date. Lastly, quantitative easing has generally been ineffective in a timorous global economy, as it is contingent on financial institutions to permeate what credit has been created.

OPEN MARKET OPERATIONS:

Central banks can also influence the supply of money directly, through buying and selling bonds from banks. To expand the money supply, it purchases bonds, which reduces short term interest rates and increases the demand for money. Therefore to contract the money supply it buys bonds, reducing the demand for money. Whilst this policy has a relatively immediate impact on economic activity, it is often subject to limitations.

As we have seen, there is no certainty nor guarantee that open market operations can change the mentality of banks, as borrowing and lending are often contingent on economic climate. Furthermore, it is easier to sell bonds as opposed to purchasing them, so to circumvent such an issue in the contemporary economy, central banks often create credit, which is essentially an extension of quantitative easing. Lastly, open market operations only influence the short term interest rate, which means that it is not a resolution for a long term problem.

RESERVE REQUIREMENTS:

Central banks can also adjust a banks reserve requirement, instead of injecting more credit into the economy through quantitative easing. We know that $M_1 = MB \times m$ (money multiplier), and since 'm' is equal to 1/reserve requirement, we also know that by increasing the reserve rate, central banks are able to proportionally reduce the money multiplier and consequently the overall money supply.

Reserve ratio's are often maintained at low rates, allowing banks to sustain an aggressive interest based fractional reserve system using a large proportion of deposits. In fact, reserve requirements are not a global policy and in many cases, they are weakly enforced. Credit creation through interest based loaning under the fractional reserve system is an issue in itself and it is not sufficient to limit this activity through weak monetary policy, rather it must be eradicated it completely.

ISLAMIC MONETARY POLICY:

In the Islamic economic system, interest has been categorically forbidden. It is impermissible for one to loan out money on condition that the borrower is to pay the principal and more (interest). This is supported by many textual evidences. The following verse, best delineates this particular issue and the severity of dealing with usury in an Islamic economy:

Allah (ﷻ) says in the Holy Quran: *"Those who devour (take) interest (riba) cannot stand except as the one whom the Satan, by (his) touch, drives him to madness. That is because they say: Trade is just like riba, whereas Allah permitted trade and forbade riba. The one to whom an admonition from his Lord comes and he refrains (in obedience thereto), he shall keep (the profits of) that which is past, and his affair (henceforth) is with Allah. As for him who returns (to usury), such are rightful owners of the fire. They will abide therein eternally."*[49]

This should be the starting point for the Muslim believer rather than appraising the rational advantages and disadvantages of interest as an economic policy/concept. That being said, to remove interest from the economic equation is to remove many illnesses within the economy. It would reduce the debt burden on borrowers which would prevent many from defaulting. Replacing interest based agreements with definitive contracts would allow economic agents (particularly investors) to make efficient decisions in the long run rather than being deterred by fluctuating rates that alter with economic climate.

Islam would chain profit to real output so as to not misconstrue the economy's performance unlike interest, which chains profit to no real output. Furthermore, the Islamic economy would not be subject to the cyclical effort in stabilising both interest and or inflation rates through monetary policy, which tend to complicate the market and often create uncertainty. In fact, due to the adoption of a classical gold standard, society (and primarily investors) needn't worry about either interest or price volatility, for the former is non-existent and the latter is easy to

Quran, 2:275 [49]

maintain at a low rate due to the nature of a commodity backed currency. Moreover, with the total abolition of interest, Islam would secure both the present and the future with a natural rate of activity as opposed to accelerated consumption in the present. Both investors and households would also have a much lower propensity to save, thus allowing for a higher circular flow of income and subsequently higher levels of growth.

As for adjusting the money supply through quantitative easing, reserve requirements and the repurchase rate; these policies do not exist under Islam as it is the bimetallic standard that restricts credit manipulation. Here, the lack of policy is not indicative of a weaker system, rather a stronger one. Through such a currency (whose benefits have already been discussed), the associated effects of the fiat are eradicated along with the failed monetary policies that seek to influence its supply. This is not to say that the state is unable to influence the economy. In order to alter the bimetallic supply, the Islamic economic system would merely need to buy/sell specie, invest/divest in mining/minting industries, et cetera. These policies can be technically defined as Islamic monetary policy, as they seek to control the supply of the bimetallic system.

To conclude, capitalist monetary policy is an ineffective tool to cure the economy in the long run. This is because it is a mechanism to treat the symptoms of an issue as opposed to its root cause. Contrastingly, Islam is an effective economic system that remedies all of the aforementioned monetary problems that capitalist policy attempts to resolve.

IX. THE FINANCIAL SECTOR

Synopsis: *The financial sector bleeds wealth from the real economy. As a result of a casino mentality, financial markets have become increasingly unstable and susceptible to crises.*

In 2008, capitalism experienced a harsh financial crisis that shook the global economy. As a result of heavy deregulation born from the fundamentals of the free market, investment banks were able to make risky trades in exchange for supernormal profit. Many have claimed that this laxity first incepted in 1998 when the Glass-Steagall act was repealed, effectively giving the banking sector a green light to gamble financial assets.[50] However, it is now clear that this issue is systemic and that such a policy only delayed the inevitable.

In the run up to the crisis, low interest rates (that were primarily remnants of the dot-com bust), essentially reduced the cost of borrowing for investors, which subsequently inflated an asset bubble. Wall Street seized this opportunity of rising asset prices on Main Street by bundling mortgages into CDO's and selling them off to investors for hefty profits. In fact, some (like the Lehman Brothers) took on a lot of debt in acts of leverage to gamble on prices within the financial market. After a sub-prime mortgage crisis swept the United States of America, economies around the world fell into a major panic. Before anyone could react to the shock, a vicious liquidity crunch began to plague the global economy, pushing it into steep decline.

It is now understood that during the boom, banks maximised their profits through risky finance and at the first sign of a recession, they hedged their trades so as to minimise loss. Hitherto, a total of $12.6 trillion is estimated to have been used to fix only the US economy.[51] What many have failed to realise is that the precursor to such crises is due to a systemic flaw in liberal capitalism as opposed to economic regulation or deregulation, and that this error has engendered a parasitic financial system that will forever erode the real economy.

Rickards, 2012 [50]

Atkinson, Luttrell and Rosenblum, 2013 [51]

FINANCIAL MARKETS[52]:

Markets in the financial sector are essentially places where investors/lenders and borrowers come together to exchange financial assets. The former possess funds that they are willing to invest in and or lend to other economic agents in return for a profit. The latter look to borrow funds for any given reason.

Both investors/lenders and borrowers, interact within the financial market through intermediaries known as investment banks, whom receive healthy profits by increasing the cost to borrowers through interest and taking from the returns of investors. The intermediary is of paramount importance as they facilitate a primary function of the financial system (which is to link agents together for the exchange of capital).

Financial markets are categorised by what good is being traded within them. It is therefore important to familiarise ourselves with these goods, so as to understand this topic better. It is also important to note that there are many markets within the financial sector, purely because there are many financial goods. The following list, merely attempts to provide a general overview of the core markets, in which most activity occurs.

Money market: In this market, short term and highly liquid investment decisions are made between borrowers and lenders. An example of this would be between governments and companies who exchange money market instruments (all of which are essentially forms of debt) with a predetermined level of interest. Due to the nature of what is traded, returns are often low, albeit almost always guaranteed. The main financial instruments that are traded in this market are as follows:

I. Treasury bills: Short term bonds, bought at one price and cashed in at another. The interest/profit is essentially equal to the difference in purchase price and final worth. These securities hold the least risk (due to the time of their maturity) and tend to make the lowest return due to their safety and high liquidity.

II. Certificate of deposit: Timed deposits that last longer than treasury bills and have a higher investment risk as there is a greater possibility that the agent will default in the longer term. These investments are less liquid and usually tied to the investor (often from three months to five years).

III. Commercial paper: Unsecured loans that are issued on a short term basis. This is chosen as an alternative to borrowing due to the higher costs involved with banks. These financial products are also relatively low in risk.

IV. Repurchase agreements: Overnight (extremely short-term) borrowing backed by government securities. These securities have been discussed in the previous chapter.

Capital market: In this market, savings and investment based securities are transferred from suppliers of capital (retail/institutional investors) to buyers/users of capital (governments, businesses and individuals). Here agents commit to longer contracts and consequently a higher risk. Activity within capital markets can occur either in the primary market where companies issue new stocks and bonds or in the secondary market where existing securities are traded. Economists also claim that the size of a countries capital market is directly proportional to the size of its economy. The main financial products that are sold/bought can be split into the following:

I. Equity based securities: These usually manifest in stocks and shares, which are bought by investors and sold by companies with the objective of raising capital.

II. Debt based securities: These usually manifest in bonds (that are akin to tradable debt), which can be bought, sold and cashed out at a later date with interest.

Commodity market: In this market, buyers and sellers interact to trade commodities and or to speculate on them. There are however, various types of commodities that are traded and they can be generally split into the following three categories:

I. Hard commodities: Raw metals such as copper, led, nickel, aluminium, gold, silver, platinum and palladium.

II. Soft commodities: Goods related to agriculture such as sugar, soybeans, coffee, corn and wheat.

III. Energy based commodities: Natural resources that must be mined/extracted such as oil, rubber and coal.

In this market, price levels can often be volatile due to the nature of commodities. Unlike stocks and shares, lenders of capital cannot easily contain the risks affiliated with commodity based products, for they are perishable, subject to environmental changes and even political climate. Trading in this market can be split into the wholesale and retail sector. In the former, investors trade large quantities of commodities, whilst in the latter, investors either purchase physical products or trade stocks/shares (that are linked to the commodity market) so as to profit from fluctuating prices.

Derivatives market: Derivatives are essentially products that derive their value from changes in the future price of another underlying entity. These underlying entities are vast and can take the form of practically anything. In each of the aforementioned markets, we find that trading often occurs in respect to derivatives rather than real assets. Ultimately, derivatives have two primary functions that we must keep in mind; they can be used for speculation or for hedging risks.

Speculation is a process by which investors trade capital based on an accurate guess of the future market price in order to make a short term profit. Hedging on the other hand, is a process by which investors are able to remove future risk of devaluating financial products by either selling or hoarding so as to wait for the price level to change in their favour. Derivatives are a central part of a financial sector and although this market is astronomical in size, derivatives come in three simple yet fundamental products, by understanding each one we will be able to understand the market for derivatives:

I. **Futures/Forwards:** These are essentially contracts that oblige a buyer to purchase an asset and a seller to sell that asset at a predetermined future price and date. Consider the farmer and his crops. When a farmer is worried about environmental hazards and a fall in his harvest, he is able to enter into a future agreement with an investor. So both agents formulate a contract specifying that the farmer will sell the investor his crops at a certain price and future date, irrespective of the future market price. Although it may seem that collectively they are removing risk by securing their future, this is a speculative gamble for the investor and the farmer as the contract is based on uncertainty.

It may be that the prices change in favour of the farmer but against the investor and vice versa. So when the time comes for the farmer to sell his crops, the market price for the amount that the investor must purchase could be lower than what has been agreed upon and as a result the investor would have made a loss (as he could have purchased the same quantity of crops at a lower market price). The antithesis could also occur, where the farmer would lose out due to the opportunity cost of selling his crops when the market price is higher than expected (as he could have sold the same quantity of crops at a higher market price). These are known as forward contracts, whilst a futures contract is a financial term which involves the trade of only contracts and no real exchange of assets.

II. **Options:** In essence, options are contracts similar to those products seen in the previous example. In finance these contracts are often referred to as the derivative of a derivative, where one is essentially specifying the right to buy a particular asset at a particular strike price at a particular time in the future. Options also have an expiry date, meaning that one would need to sell it with a premium in order to profit. When one agent sells this option to another, the outcome and risk attached to it (as we saw previously) is transferred to the buyer.

This may seem like an easy way to exit a futures contract but in reality it is a <u>gamble</u> for both agents involved, as it may be that prices change in favour/against the trader who acquires the option and or the one who sells it. It is clear that volatility is ultimately being traded here in the form of an option; the higher the volatility the more expensive the security in question, due to the higher risk involved.

III. **Swaps:** These contracts involve two agents exchanging financial instruments such as interest rates, derivatives or even securities (like stocks and bonds). Although this section is based on derivatives, let us use the simplest form of a swap to better understand the product. By doing this, we can apply the same concept to a derivative.

Consider the following example, involving an interest rate swap to reduce borrowing costs: Company A has a high credit rating and wishes to take out a loan at a variable interest rate. Company B has a lower credit rating and wishes to take out a loan at a fixed interest rate. As a result of their credit ratings, banks are able to discriminate against them by charging different interest rates.

Swap banks offer a way of reducing interest for both companies whilst also making a profit in the process. In this case, the intermediary advises company A to borrow against its will with a fixed interest rate and advises company B to borrow against its will with a variable (often LIBOR) interest rate. By swapping contracts between both agents, each become better off. This is what is known as a gain from comparative advantage. Banks profit from raising/lowering the interest by a small amount so as to profit during the swap. The same mechanism can also be applied to a different instrument, in this case derivatives. It may seem efficient but derivative swaps are a <u>gamble,</u> as the risk attached is merely shifted/swapped from one agent to another and these swaps are also subject to 'bilateral risk', where one agent is at risk of the other defaulting.

IMPACTS ON THE REAL ECONOMY:

As we have seen, capitalism is composed of two main sectors. The 'real sector' is all that we notice around us, from the tangible goods to the intangible services. It is concerned with the actual production of goods and services. Contrastingly, the 'financial sector' was designed to serve the real economy by facilitating investment, payments, savings and risk distribution. Many economists firmly believe that this sector is a necessary part of contemporary capitalist states, as it allows the physical exchange of capital on a large and efficient basis. Let us take a look at some of the true effects that the capitalist based financial sector has on the real economy:

Growth: By syphoning out funds from the real economy and circulating them in the financial sector through securities and financial instruments, capitalism has created financial growth as opposed to real activity. In fact, the total size of the global financial market in 2014 sat at $156 trillion, more than twice the size of global gross domestic product (real growth).[53a] If one were to include the market for securitised products, this figure would rise to $200 trillion and that is still discounting the astronomically large derivatives market.[53b] Capital is no longer being used to kindle the physical transfer of wealth but to trade instruments and securities for profit with no intention of moving real assets. As a result, financial markets bleed wealth from the real economy by hampering real production in exchange for unsubstantiated gain. Little wealth from this profit has actually permeated to the real economy and society has subsequently accrued a massive opportunity cost.

Credit: If we look to financial markets after the crisis, we find that banks have consistently traded safer government-backed securities as opposed to making credit available to the public in the form of loans, primarily due to a lack of confidence. This has resulted in a liquidity crisis whereby credit within the economy is failing to stimulate aggregate demand. In fact, the only growth that seems to be occurring is in the bond market itself. As such, financial markets have ultimately given banks a very lucrative alternative to loaning, which has subsequently reduced household expenditure, stifled aggregate demand in the real economy and caused an overall decline in productivity.

Risk: Asset markets in general have harboured gamblers who continue to use wealth from the real economy to speculate on volatile prices in order to multiply profits. Lehman Brothers exemplified this by borrowing billions to gamble on pure speculation (particularly on mortgages).[54] After bankruptcy, they initiated a chain reaction in the asset market, causing mass defaults amongst other financial institutions (who also engaged in leverage). As a result, the real economy suffered drastically; house prices declined, pension funds diminished, savings were afflicted and illiquidity rose. The risks that these casino markets are grounded on are clearly unsustainable. Cracks within the framework of capitalism have caused tremors to society and whilst its structure currently remains intact, the current financial system makes collapse an increasingly likely prospect.

Private debt: The Bank of International Settlements (BIS) revealed that the debt market grew to $100 trillion in 2014.[55] Such a figure is indicative of the interest based debt system that capitalism exploits. The McKinsey study also proved that not a single major economy has deleveraged their debt to GDP ratio. The report also states that this debt level has grown by $57 trillion since 2007.[56] The real sector has gradually become highly dependant on debt to progress due to the models used by the banking sector. As we will see, high private debt is a precursor to defaults, impoverishment and above all, crises.

Societal burden: The financial market may have once been designed to sustain the real economy but the roles in this relationship have reversed. The financial market has repeatedly stabbed the real economy, withdrawing large sums of wealth from it. To make matters worse, post financial crisis, society has had to pick up the pieces of the bust whilst banks and the financial sector remained totally immune from admonishment.

---

[54] Sandler, 2011
[55] Gruić and Schrimpf, 2014
[56] Roxburgh, Lund and Piotrowsk, 2011   93

Governments have globally bailed out many institutions with hard earned taxpayer funds from suffocating austerity measures purely to keep capitalism from capitulating. Whilst the real sector continues to suffer from budget cuts, the perpetrators have lost little and have yet to see any form of accountability or punishment. Their activity in the financial sector has rapidly grown since 2008 and it is only time that history repeats itself.

Derivatives: The market for derivatives is the epitome of just how fragile capitalism is and what it could potentially inflict on the real economy. High estimates suggest that this casino market has grown to a staggering notional value of $1.5 quadrillion.[57] Rightly so, the iconic investor Warren Buffet viewed "derivatives as time bombs" and called them "financial weapons of mass destruction."[58] Speculation, risk based trading and high debt in this market were the main causes to the most recent crisis and whilst capitalism has a history of saving itself with the real economy, the idea that it can use it again is gradually decaying. The exponential growth in the derivatives market is a clear indication of this dwindling prospect.

Prices: As a result of rampant speculation on financial assets, essential goods within the commodity market such as oil, iron, grain and wheat, have all been subject to price volatility. This is not caused by sudden changes in demand, rather by hoarders of wealth whom seek to profit in the future. As a result, society forgoes large sums of real wealth that is compounded into the financial sector, which widens inequality as commodities (in ownership) are reserved in the pockets of a few as opposed to being distributed to the rest of society. This phenomenon is not restricted to the commodity market, rather any matter that is speculated on, such as house prices in the form of mortgages.

Confidence: The real economy has suffered a great deal from the recent financial crisis. This has painted a bleak, gloomy and depressing image for the average household and indeed for the whole economy. Harsher austerity measures, higher debt levels, volatile prices, poor investment prospects, massive inequality,

Snyder, 2014 [57]
Buffet, 2002 [58]

ineffective resource distribution, failed policies and devaluating currencies along with many other negative phenomena that currently exist within the capitalist system, have reduced confidence to an absolute minimum. This is a major concern within the financial sector, as investors do not want to engage in projects due to uncertainties in return, whilst households are simultaneously reluctant to inject their wealth into financial institutions that heavily depend on it. The lack of confidence is currently holding back credit within banks and widening the disparity between the money supply and growth. In actuality, confidence is what underpins most economic activity and so the behaviour of agents is critical to maintain, so as to preserve the real economy. Unfortunately, capitalism has failed to achieve this objective (of maintaining long term economic confidence) and has consequently thrown stability out of the equation.

MINSKY'S FINANCIAL INSTABILITY HYPOTHESIS:

American economist Hyman Minsky was a core contributor to the explanations behind financial crises. Indeed, in the same manner that Irving Fisher advanced the theory of debt deflation, Minsky developed a strong position on the precursor to financial crises by explaining how certain agents actively push the economy into decline. His financial instability hypothesis has become a crucial talking point in economic discourse as he was amongst the very few who provided an explanation to the crisis of 2008 in 1992.[59] In fact, Minsky tendentiously stated, that such crises were endemic in capitalism due to the cyclical transition from stability to instability.

If we recall, when discussing the fractional reserve system, this book highlighted inconsistencies in the outdated model adopted by most economists. This orthodox view assumed that savings were a direct transfer of wealth from savers to borrowers. This meant that the agent who saved more would spend less and the agent who received what was saved would spend more, hence inferring an equilibrium. We noted that this was inaccurate as it failed to explain our reality. Ensuing this, we looked at a second model, which explicated the fractional reserve system and

---

[59] Minsky, 1992

although it was a useful foundation, we found it to be based on two major assumptions. The first was of a passive banking sector and the second was that the central bank had full control over the money supply. This book then concluded that banks created credit according to economic climate and that this credit reflected debt in exactly the same proportion.

Hyman Minsky's hypothesis is therefore not grounded on a false banking model, rather it can be used to understand the financial sector for what it is and how it truly functions.[60] Indeed, if loans are essentially debt that are used for spending, debt must also factor into aggregate demand. Minsky explains this concept and how total aggregate demand is not purely measured by what goods and services are produced but also by the change in debt level. In fact, before the financial crisis, total private debt was multiple times the level of GDP. This was a problem for society as it meant that banks had an inherent bias to create more debt in order to profit and to stimulate the economy further. To make matters worse, banks themselves had a pro-leverage mentality which only added to the instability.

So how does an economy transition from one state (of stability) to another (of instability)? At times of expansion in growth and inflation, both lenders and borrowers have a higher tendency to become optimistic and to inherit greater risk. This predilection for risk at times of economic prosperity, pushes the financial sector to engage in more leverage based trade. At the same time, financial institutions lure individuals into debt, by selling them the idea that asset prices will continue rise in the future. Minsky refers to these agents as 'Ponzi' financiers who profit by selling assets on rising markets.

As a result of this price illusion, the borrower is fooled by the bank who offers the loan with an expectation of a profit. Consequently the increased demand for the underlying asset drives up prices and this ultimately becomes a self fulfilling mechanism. This positive chain (of borrowing and a subsequent return) attracts more borrows to the market who also seek to profit, which causes a speculative asset bubble and as a result,

Keen, 2014 [60]

investment bankers and the real estate agents trading these financial products make larger interest based gain. According to Minsky, as this irrational exuberance continues, aggregate demand increases but debt rises at a faster rate and once it passes the event horizon by outstripping aggregate demand, it becomes impossible to finance, causing the entire economy to collapse mainly due to mass default and illiquidity.[61a]

In summary the financial instability hypothesis developed by the notable economist Hyman Minsky, begins on the pretext of a "euphoric economy" where asset prices are rising and speculation in the financial market on these assets becomes profitable.[61b] This invites more borrowers to enter the market so as to profit from these rising asset prices, which signals a higher profit for banks and a higher risk for investors. As a result of the rising debt level and interest on loans, borrowers are unable to service their costs and default, bursting the speculative bubble. This forces a wave of deleveraging, a rapid reduction in the level of aggregate demand and illiquidity due to the fear that loans will not be repaid in the future. Indeed, this hypothesis clearly outlines the dangers of the debt based finance system and alludes to a need for an alternative.

Many have praised this hypothesis in its capacity to explain the most recent financial crisis of 2008. In fact, economists began to refer to the crisis as a 'Minsky moment', when economies began to transition from stability to instability. Economist Paul McCulley drew the comparisons between the hypothesis and the credit crisis by claiming that the primary culprit was an unstable financial sector that ultimately collapsed due to the aforementioned reasons given by professor Hyman Minsky.[62]

Before the crisis, interest rates were extremely low, which attracted agents on Wall Street to borrow large sums of credit, in acts of leverage, to profit from mortgages on Main Street. In this scenario, Minsky's theory explains how borrowers are disillusioned due to already rising asset prices and the incentive to make a return in the future.

---

[61] Minsky, 1992
[62] McCulley, 1998

Lenders then offered these mortgage contracts to investment bankers who purchased and combined many of them to form a large portfolio of consistent returns. These contracts were then split according to their risk (high risk with high rates of return, medium risk with average rates of return and low risk with low rates of return), these products were then formally labelled a collateralised debt obligation or CDO. Hence, by repackaging these contracts, investment bankers were able to sell them under a false risk rating. Triple A rated contracts went to investors, triple B rated contracts went to other financial agents and high unrated contracts went to risk takers.

After the fast growth in debt and aggregate demand towards 2008, lenders began to run out of qualified homeowners to lend to and in order to maintain their return under the climate of prosperity, financial agents began to add more risk, which meant handing out mortgages to less responsible families (sub-prime) as opposed to responsible ones (prime). Due to defaults on these, sub-prime mortgages, the supply of houses in the market rose, causing prices to naturally fall. Mortgage holders at the time canceled their payments as their houses devaluated in real terms, which ultimately caused a downwards spiral in the value of risk based derivatives that were essentially pushed around in the financial sector. As a result of the astronomical financial debt accrued during the boom, banks stopped lending and many went bust, which lead to a decline in private debt due to deleveraging.[63] Minsky's theory is evidently applicable to the credit crisis of 2008 as it effectively explicates the reasons behind it and the process which lead to such decline.

ISLAM'S ALTERNATIVE TO CAPITALIST FINANCE:

The Islamic economic system does not contend the notion of allocating capital between agents. Indeed, to denounce the aim of the financial market would be to deny the idea of bringing capital to the entrepreneur and prospects to the investor, which is a matter that Islam condones entirely. However, as we have noticed, capitalism uses an interest based debt model in order to link capital owners to those who require the capital.

This mechanism is deconstructive as it has become a profit maximising tool as opposed to an effective way of organising investment and capital. As a result of a lack of wealth amongst the many, this system has sold the people a façade; that they may chase their dreams only through interest based debt (tied to the financial sector). As we have seen, this inequality has been kindled by credit creation and has caused mass levels of poverty due to the interest levied on society. So the dependancy on interest based debt for financing projects and ambitions is derived from core capitalist principles. However, this is only a small part of the discussion. Let us now analyse the Islamic alternative to the current financial system and its ability to solve some of the key problems mentioned in the former topics.

Equity based partnership: Islam promotes an equity based system in which the obligation of a financial intermediary is eliminated and the constant inclination towards debt is suppressed. It uproots all corruption in the current banking sector, whereby financial institutions trade real capital from society with supernormal profit. The Islamic economic system enables entrepreneurs to directly engage in profit and loss sharing contracts with the suppliers of capital so as to distribute risk equally. Islam removes the incessant tendency towards debt based finance by defining equity as the funds that originate from savings rather than loans handed out by financial intermediaries. Economic agents come together on the collective terms of pushing capital to its real use as opposed to gambling and speculation, with no intention of developing the real economy. This impartial mechanism of uniting investors with the owners of capital as opposed to the capital itself is an effective method of distributing profits amongst partners and losses upon their capital.

Incentivising finance: If we look to the contemporary financial system we find that it is grounded primarily on the wealth of society. In fact, there is an incentive for individuals within capitalism to hoard their excess capital with the intention of reaping both short term and long term profit, whether that be in the money, capital or commodity market. As an alternative,

Islam encourages the re-injection of surplus wealth through a wealth based taxation system and a prohibition against hoarding, as this causes funds within the economy to remain idle and useless. This directs capital to the real economy for real projects which further kindles employment and investment. Higher levels demand allow currency to change hands at a higher velocity whilst an equity based partnership scheme expands the range in which money is transferred.

Definitive contracts: Capital markets have reaped the real wealth of people by convincing society of 'potential' profit. For example, the problem with joint stock companies is a lack of offer and acceptance between the buyer and seller of shares. These vague contracts are not based on partnership rather risk is primarily pushed to the shareholder. There is also no subject matter upon which both agents make any agreement, in other words companies are not bound by the opinions or choices of their shareholders rather they act as free agents. This autonomy skews responsibility and leaves the shareholder out of key decisions. Ultimately massive levels of wealth are transferred to companies that give little back (in dividends) to those who hold shares in them. Islam realises the inequality in such financial activity and establishes profit and loss sharing partnerships where both agents involve themselves in projects based on agreements between the parters involved rather than their capital. These definitive contracts allow both agents to collectively share the benefits and feel the losses that they may encounter. In Islam, partners are responsible for their activity according to the contracts they have defined, which paves the way for sensible and effective market interaction.

Regulation: Islam ends the unlimited and deconstructive freedom under capitalism by monitoring and regulating the private sector, correcting the market from any activity that does not conform to the *sharia*, such as gambling. In essence, the actions of private financial institutions are akin to stealing the people's wealth only to squander it in vain, which is a matter that Muhammad (ﷺ) once commented on (an evidence upon which the obligation for regulation is built):

He said: "*The one who takes people's wealth intending to pay it back, Allah will pay it back for him, and the one who takes it intending to destroy it, Allah will destroy him.*"[64]

However, whilst regulation is the active deterrent, ethical/moral concepts act as a stimulus to prevent financial exploitation and to encourage/motivate/promote sensible trading. It is this binary mechanism that ultimately attains economic prosperity.

Gold standard: Unlike capitalism, Islam promotes a currency that eliminates price volatility. Investors will be comforted in knowing that finance is built on a stable container of value that is not subject to the whims and desires of governments or financial institutions. This facilities investment in the real economy and restores confidence amongst households. Currency lies at the heart of any economy and if it is unstable or ineffective, this will cause problems that lead to demise. Indeed, it was John Maynard Keynes who said that "the best way to destroy the capitalist system is to debauch the currency" and this is effectively what is being done by the current financial system. In fact, capitalism is the mother who gave birth to the very children (institutions) that now seek to kill her. Contrastingly, Islam secured financial activity through a debt free currency that feeds into the real economy as opposed to the financial sector. Furthermore, the gold standard protects the economy from Minsky's financial instability hypothesis as it strips away the power held by these financial institutions, to manipulate the fiat system, so as to chase interest based profit through passing on the debt to society.

Restoring confidence: This is another core issue faced by the capitalists. Due to the aforementioned negative externalities, people no longer trust the economy to deliver. As a result, pessimism is rampant within the real sector, damaging the financial sector a great deal due to the lack of motivation towards debt and spending. By reorganising this cancerous financial sector, Islam restores this confidence and protects the real economy from harm. It must be noted that this is the prescription for endogenous failure, as for exogenous shocks,

---

[64] Bukhari, ND

Islam frowns upon debt and actively encourages agents to write off what the borrower is struggling to pay. This ultimately eases the impact of any unpredictable tremors due to a lower level of aggregate liability. In fact, Islam even makes use of the *zakat* to achieve this objective. Furthermore, any shocks that do hurt the economy are distributed equally between suppliers and users of capital, as opposed to merely the shareholder.

The Islamic economic system also pumps ideas such as *rizq* (provisions) and *al-qada wal qadr* (the divine decree) into the minds of muslims, which help to combat greater economic issues such as a lack of confidence; *rizq* is an understanding that all provisions are from Allah (ﷻ) and that man is required to seek them in order to acquire them, whilst *al-qada wal qadr* essentially allows the Muslim to appreciate his sphere of influence and what he has no control over. Ultimately these concepts kindle confidence and equip the Muslims to face challenging economic climates that may arise due to various reasons, thus preserving financial activity and stability.

X. BUDGET DEFICIT AND DEBT CRISIS

Synopsis: An unrestrained growth based mentality has forced governments to accrue interest based debt in order to finance deficit spending. This habituation has created many structural problems, pushing economies into decline.

Debt plays a role in both the private and public sector of any given economy. The latter is often the result of deficit spending whilst the former is often the result of leverage within the financial sector. In contrast, a budget deficit is the negative divergence between government revenue (in taxation) and public expenditure, both of which are influenced by fiscal policy. In many instances however, such policy can be ineffective, which makes borrowing more attractive. Raising the debt ceiling is an ostensible means to fund public expenditure, for in reality, there are certain dangers affiliated with growing debt and a deteriorating budget deficit; ranging from fiscal crises to mass default.[65]

However, perhaps the greatest issue faced by society as a result of poor budgetary management is the austerity that often follows. As such, growing deficits and debt have slowly eroded societies aggregate wealth and kindled capital inequality, In fact, the developing world has suffered the most from such phenomena. This has led to an overwhelming need for policy to be externally determined by higher powers (such as the International Monetary Fund) so as to safeguard the world from default. However, this intervention has led to exploitation and inefficiency, putting society at risk with greater fiscal issues. Evidently then, this topic is pertinent to capitalism and it is a matter that Islam must dispense with.

Before explicating the Islamic solution to this issue, one must first grasp both the anatomy and severity of both a debt and deficit crisis. This chapter shall therefore focus initially on how the theoretical macroeconomy falls into the aforementioned paradigm and how this has been epitomised in reality (with reference to the European crisis).

---

[65] IFS, 2014

Let us use 'E_x' as a placeholder to denote a fictional economy, whose expenses are far beyond its income. In order to fund this deficit, E_x can make use of fiscal policy to either raise revenue or reduce expenditure. However, if E_x cuts expenditure through harsh austerity measures, the people who it is spending on would suffer, inadvertently reducing the standard of living and hindering the economy due to lower levels of aggregate demand. On the other hand, if E_x raises the tax level, stakeholders (firms, households, et cetera) would have less money to spend, which would reduce consumption and could even lead to dissension. It would also bring in lower tax revenues as shown on the Laffer curve, originally invented by Ibn Khaldun in his book 'Muqaddimah' (see appendix X).

As an alternative to fiscal policy, governments often borrow to maintain their spending. However, high debt (or even sustained borrowing) erodes investment due to a lack of confidence in the governments ability to maintain repayment, ultimately leading to declining aggregate demand. Furthermore, E_x cannot persistently borrow as creditors often push up the interest rate, due to the collateral and a rise in risk (of default). In light of this, E_x contemplates (and often commits) to a route that does not upset any of the aforementioned stakeholders in the short run; that is to create credit. However, even this manoeuvre causes monetary inflation in the long run (the effects of which have been discussed extensively in previous chapters).

The only option thereafter, is to take out more loans even if E_x is unable to pay back its present ones. In other words, a dependency on debt to maintain expenditure, leads to economic recidivism and increases the chances of a debt spiral. Inevitably there will come a time in the future when the debt level becomes insurmountable. When this occurs, and when lenders refuse to leak anymore credit, stakeholders will not receive money to pay for their loans/bills/payments (all of whom also circulate debt/loans/bonds). When investors are unable to pay their fees, corporations cannot pay their workers, when banks are unable to pay their bills, consumers cannot take out loans due to illiquidity or even withdraw money from their bank account. If foreign countries are unable to pay their fees/bills, they too will suffer the same aforementioned fate and if the debt pile is large enough (in that it is shared and of a mammoth quantity), this sovereign debt crisis could have a global impact.

THE EUROPEAN CRISIS:

Although the aforementioned scenario is an extreme case of what a debt crisis could potentially morph into, one can learn a great deal about the practical manifestations of capital imbalances from the ongoing 'European Crisis'.

Pre-WWII, Europe suffered from endemic internal conflict, which resulted in many barriers that hindered both investment and trade. These obstructions mainly came in the form of tariffs and exchange rates. After the war however, 27 European countries united under the 'Maastricht Treaty' to abolish trade barriers for collective economic growth.[66] Furthermore, on the 1st of January 1999, they established a single currency called the 'euro' (€) and thereafter, the eurozone was born. One of the major outcomes of this agreement was the abolishment of individual domestic monetary policy and the establishment of a European Central Bank on the 1st of June 1998.

As a result of this economic integration, countries within the Eurozone began to converge; interconnected markets promoted trade, competition began to rise and with the introduction of a single currency, inflation and interest rates seemed to converge. [67] However, this period of prosperity came to an abrupt end and was short-lived by the financial crisis. In fact, unlike the United States (from which the shock originated), Europe was relatively less exposed, yet it suffered badly and still does today. Conventional analysis has often blamed deteriorating budget deficits and public indebtedness as the root cause to the crisis. However, the notion that fiscal imbalances were the sole cause to European disintegration is entirely fictitious.

---

[66] Panarella, 1995
[67] Praussello, 2012

Whilst it certainly played an important role in countries like Greece and Portugal, others like Ireland actually maintained a surplus. In actuality, the EU's failure can be statistically traced to external imbalances before the crisis, whereby current accounts and international investment positions began to deteriorate amongst periphery countries (i.e Portugal, Italy, Greece and Spain). In fact, they maintained the highest current account deficits and external indebtedness, both of which grew rapidly after the Euro's introduction.

Further still, capital seemed to move from the periphery to the core (i.e Germany, France, Belgium, et cetera). This is better understood through the Solow-Swan Model (see appendix XI), whereby core countries essentially looked unto the periphery as profitable due to low levels of capital and high levels of potential productivity. The sharp rise in investment from core savings, meant that the periphery began to grow and converge, engendering a boom. Credit and debt circulated the eurozone, locking the fate of each country tightly together. As variables like wages and prices rose, productivity diminished and the boom, backed largely by leverage, began to slow down. The scales were finally tipped post financial crisis, when investors immediately grew risk averse and capital stopped flowing into the periphery, which prevented them from financing their current account deficits. It is at this point where the European project became more a dream than a potential reality.

Portugal, Italy, Greece and Spain, lured on by low interest rates, also made a number of fiscal promises to its people (such as more jobs and higher pensions). As discussed earlier, when faced with debt maturity many of these economies simply took more loans out to renew old ones, rather than using fiscal policy to either cut expenditure and or raise taxation. After the crisis of 2008, banks stopped lending due to bankruptcy fears, which meant that countries like Greece failed to sustain their debt driven promises (because of illiquidity). As a result of the a tightly intertwined eurozone, issues faced by the periphery economies spread into core countries and when many were on the brink of collapse, the strongest amongst them (Germany), agreed to bailout the debtor (periphery) nations under harsh austerity conditions. Whilst the reasons behind such a crises are often debated, it is certainly clear that external imbalances had a core role in the eurozone's decline. Over time, policymakers have focused primarily on the symptoms as opposed to the root cause insofar as countries like Greece and Portugal have been made weary of their fiscal excesses as opposed to their external imbalances. In fact, cooperation and credibility could have also mitigated the European crisis; by pursuing expansionary policy, core countries like Germany could have increased the flow of capital into the periphery so as to improve their current account balance, thus dampening the European slowdown.

PRIVATE VERSUS PUBLIC DEBT:

Hitherto, we have discussed the nature of debt and the impact it can have on the overall economy. Whilst this debt itself is an important consideration, many economists often focus purely on public sector debt as opposed to that which exists within the private sector. This is a naïve misjudgment, which also led to the demise of Greece. Private debt is essentially defined as debt held by privately owned institutions such as banks, financial institutions, households, firms, businesses, et cetera. If we recall the previous chapter, it was an escalating level of private debt that financed the asset bubble (primarily in the form of leverage), which ultimately led to mass default. In fact, one could say that it was a private debt crisis that ultimately induced financial instability, engendering the bust of 2008.[68]

Rightly so, some economists firmly believe that private debt is an even greater issues than sovereign debt as it directly effects individuals, households and businesses. This debt is primarily generated in the financial sector, where institutions leverage funds to gamble on prices. Growing debt ultimately mean that agents will be unable to finance their repayments in the future, which will inevitably initiate yet another spiral of default. In fact, statistics released by the Institute for Fiscal Studies post crisis, demonstrated this very point (of private debt).[69]

---

[68] ONS, 2014
[69] IFS, 2008

In 1999, Spain had a public debt to GDP ratio of 60% and a private debt to GDP ratio of 80; in 2007, the former fell to roughly 30% whilst the latter shot up to 180%. In 1999, Ireland had a public debt to GDP ratio of 50% and a private debt to GDP ratio of 100%; in 2007, the former fell to 25% whilst the latter rose to 200%. In 1999, Portugal had a public debt to GDP ratio of 50% and a private debt to GDP ratio of approximately 105%; in 2007, the former rose to 60% whilst the latter rose to 160%. Finally, in 1999, Greece had a public debt to GDP ratio of 100% and a private debt to GDP ratio of about 55%; in 2007, the former rose to roughly 102% whilst the latter increased to almost 90%. These statistics prove that private debt outweighed public debt pre and post crisis. It is also clear that such poison was a precursor to it, especially from defaults within the financial sector, as the average level of debt rose substantially between 1999 and 2007, only to climax in 2008, before financial institutions deleveraged their financial obligations.

ISLAM'S CURE TO DEFICIT AND DEBT:

The Islamic economic system preempts the aforementioned precursors to a sovereign debt crisis by dealing with each of them prematurely. Evidently, insuperable deficits lead to a vicious debt cycle, due to the fear of using fiscal policy. The Islamic economic system ensures that deficits are a rare phenomenon by virtue of efficient fiscal policy and preventative measures. One must note that there are two sides to this capitalist problem; one is the inability of governments to raise funds for spending and the other is a predilection for falling into a deficit in the first instance.

The former would seldom transpire under the Islamic economic system, as funds for a deficit are raised primarily through an effective, wealth based taxation system. This is a scheme that is stable, insofar as the amount of tax does not vary to a large degree and it is sustainable, insofar as economic agents will be less disgruntled paying them due to relatively lower rates (which would mean consistent tax receipts). As we will see in the next chapter, if governments maintain an effective taxation system that appropriately equalises wealth, incidence would be heavier on the rich as opposed to the poor, unlocking more funds for the state to manage problems such as a budget deficit.

Furthermore, capitalism has actively circulated the concept of benefit maximisation and cost minimisation, giving agents a lucrative incentive to manipulate the current tax system. Tax avoidance has become a major issue when governments are trying to pay off their budget deficits as these funds contribute to expected revenues. To make matters worse, exploiting tax loopholes is not always illegal but just within the law. In Islam however, the act of both avoiding and evading tax (which harshly affects government deficit payments) is treated as an act of rebellion and it is responded to accordingly. In fact, the Caliph can actively force payments from those who are clearly in a position to pay but refuse to do so.

This is certainly antithetical to the free market, that grants major corporations and wealthy individuals the autonomy to act freely, even if it means avoiding/evading taxation. In fact, capitalism maintains many taxes that take more from the poor in society (whom are a majority with little wealth) as opposed to the rich (whom are a minority with vast wealth), which has consequently led to poor t tax receipts. In contrast, the Islamic economy is able to fund a large percentage of its deficit from tax revenues, due to the aforementioned scheme that squeezes the pockets of the rich more so than those of the poor.

The main problems often associated with contractionary fiscal policy are negative externalities that pose a threat to society in the form of lower aggregate demand and more conservative households. But as we have learnt in previous chapters, an Islamic society is much more resilient to shocks such as necessary spending cuts, due to unique Islamic concepts, making fiscal policy a more attractive option. Evidently then, the Islamic economic system deals with issues before they arise so as to prevent their effects, by making sure deficits do not transpire and that the tax system is operational, effective and more importantly, abided by. The Islamic economy maintains a set form of fiscal policy stipulated by the *sharia* and it does not give autonomy to individual provinces to manipulate it. As we have seen, weak fiscal regulation contributed to the European crisis and gave countries the ability to borrow freely, causing them to be highly dependant on debt so as to fund expenditure.

As for the latter issue (of a tendency to fall into a deficit), this would also be rare, as fiscal imbalances between revenues and expenditure, arise mainly from obligatory spending at times of crises and are not a naturally recurring phenomenon. This is because Islam prioritises equity over growth, and hence unlike capitalism, the economy would not require perpetual fiscal stimulus (beyond its means) to achieve and or maintain a high growth rate. Furthermore, the Caliph and his committee are obliged to spend what is within the means of the Muslim body, in a sagacious and prudent manner. This is kindled by Islamic concepts such as an accountability towards Allah (ﷻ) and a duty towards the people, whilst it is also concomitantly enforced by a group, known formally as the *Mahkamat al-Madhalim* (The Court of Unjust Acts), whose very purpose is to account the Caliph and to straighten him if he becomes crooked, even in respect to the states expenditure. Thus government spending is considered in Islam, a responsibility of paramount importance, upon which he is held accountable.

On the issue of debt, it is clear that both private and public agents under capitalism often finance their spending/investment by borrowing large sums of wealth, whereas in Islam, financial obligations are often seen as a burden on the shoulder of the one who carries them and a matter which is taken to the grave. In fact, on this matter, Muhammad (salutations and peace be upon him) is reported to have supplicated to Allah the Almighty over this matter in the following prayer: "*O Allah, I seek refuge with You from sin and heavy debt.*"[70]

In this regard, any debt should be paid back with great urgency, and as for dealing with the problem proactively, Islam strips and replaces the current financial model that is founded on an incessant need to borrow with an equity based partnership

         Al-Bukhari, ND [70]

system. In addition to this, it raises the standard of living through its successful mechanism of distributing wealth as opposed to storing it in the pockets of the highest echelon in society, which reduces inequality and the need for the lower class to borrow in order to invest. The motivation for a debt free economy is best encapsulated in the following evidence:

Muhammad (ﷺ) once said: *"By the One in Whose hand is my soul, if a man were killed in battle for the sake of Allah, then brought back to life, then killed and brought back to life again, then killed, and he owed a debt, he would not enter Paradise until his debt was paid off."*[71]

Islam actively encourages writing off debt for the one who is unable or struggling to repay with the revenues made from *zakat*. This is not to say it incentivises moral hazard by protecting debtors, rather it assesses the matter appropriately and takes relevant action, contributing to long term stability due to less insolvency and a lower level of debt dependency.

Finally, Islam locates the source of this entire issue in a growth based mentality, which convinces people that an economy with debt but accelerated growth is better than an economy with no debt and a natural growth rate. In fact, Karl Marx refers to capitalism's relentless process of overcoming limitation (which in this case is analogous to the threat of lower growth), in the latter parts of The Grundrisse. He writes that capitalism cannot abide limits, but can only work "assiduously to convert them into barriers that can be transcended or by-passed", as if to deceive the people by claiming that reality has ameliorated, when in actuality, it continues to collapse.[72]

Contrastingly, the Islamic economic system places primacy upon distribution as opposed to growth (although it does not neglect the latter), which consequently eliminates the need for debt to artificially push up gross domestic product. This is what ultimately drives an economy away from deficit spending and a poor budget towards financial prosperity and fiscal success.

---

[71] Al-Nasa'i, ND
[72] Harvey, 2010

DEBT STATISTICS[73]:   Data recorded on 12.02.2015

- Global public debt currently stands at $60,642,731,625,837 and it is rising at $76,858 per second.

- US: National debt is $18,132,398,223,019 (104.85% of GDP) rising at $45,486 per second. Budget deficit is -4.6% of GDP. Debt per citizen is $57,018. Annual interest is $525,650,424,225.

- China: National debt is ¥32,574,137,475,427 (63.03% of GDP) rising at ¥34,717 per second. Budget deficit is -2.3% of GDP. Debt per citizen is ¥24,040. Annual interest is ¥1,094,839,684,954.

- Japan: National debt is ¥1,205,084,343,117,309 (199% of GDP) rising at ¥490,390 per second. Budget deficit is -6.7% of GDP. Debt per citizen is ¥9,470,957. Annual interest is ¥15,464,941,656,138.

- Germany: National debt is €2,649,760,704,510 (80.89% of GDP) rising at €1,556 per second. Budget deficit is 0.2% of GDP. Debt per citizen is €32,412. Annual interest is €61,922,732,940.

- UK: National debt is £1,593,340,880,851 (86.14% of GDP) rising at £5,170 per second. Budget deficit is -4.1% of GDP. Debt per citizen is £24,627. Annual interest is £45,249,364,901.

- France: National debt is €2,184,331,069,481 (99.15% of GDP) rising at €1,704 per second. Budget deficit is -4.0% of GDP. Debt per citizen is €33,029. Annual interest is €53,728,386,832.

- India: National debt is ₹57,014,573,637,181 (49.35% of GDP) rising at ₹138,432 per second. Budget deficit is -5.9% of GDP. Debt per citizen is ₹44,929. Annual interest is ₹4,365,602,078,605.

XI. FISCAL POLICY

Synopsis: Fiscal authorities under the capitalist system have made society worse off due to weak tax structures, poor expenditure policies and harsh austerity measures.

Fiscal policy is related to both government revenue and public expenditure. Whilst most funds for the latter originate from taxation, a large portion also comes from borrowing and even government-led devices. Tax receipts are, in essence, meant to be re-injected back into the economy, so as to sustain and or kindle it. Whilst this may be the objective, it is certainly not a concrete reality. In fact, over capitalism's existence, society has often witnessed the wastage of wealth in great extremes at the behest of both politicians and economists; from bailing out elite investment banks to funding chaotic military expeditions. As a result of such irresponsibility, the trust placed in governments to use the people's wealth responsibly has gradually eroded.

In 2013 HM Revenues and Customs announced a tax deficit of £35bn.[74a] This is essentially the difference between expected tax returns and receipts. It was also reported that £5.1bn had been lost due to tax evasion, £4.7bn due to fraud and £4bn due to tax avoidance through financial loopholes.[74b] From 2011 to 2012, £11.4bn of total VAT, £15.3bn of total income tax, £4.7bn of total corporation tax, and roughly £2.5bn excise duties failed to be collected.[74c] These figures are a small part of a larger historical record, which show a consistent loss in tax revenues that have ultimately contributed to the UK's budget deficit.

Tax systems have also caused a large uproar within capitalist societies, due to the staggering polarity between what is taken from the people and what is kept by them. For example, in 2014 it was reported that British workers took roughly 57.28% of their income, whilst in the same year, their American co-workers took home a slightly higher average of 60.45%.[75] To make matters even worse, direct and progressive income based taxation is perhaps the main cause of capital inequality.

---

[74] Syal, 2013
[75] Carter, 2014

Statistically speaking, the Equality Trust reported that "the poorest 10% of households pay eight percentage points more of their income in all taxes than the richest 43%".[76] Such inequity is primarily due to weak tax structures that are regularly abused and exploited by the rich and wealthy through financial and legislative loopholes. As such, capitalism has failed the people, in that it only seeks to accumulate funds without caring for the method by which this is done.

As for government (public) expenditure, it is clear that post Keynesianism, spending has often been at its highest after an economic contraction. In fact, after the financial crisis, we saw a consistent divergence between expenditure and income due to deficit spending, which ultimately translated into higher levels of debt and tougher austerity measures so as to recuperate the imbalance. Indeed, empirical data has proven that spending is necessary to prevent stagnation and to revive those that have suffered from the brunt of a bust. However, this point becomes entirely redundant upon realising that the bust itself was preventable, saving the public the great burden of sustaining high levels of expenditure.

Such recidivism is a common theme under capitalism, one that has cost the people a great amount of wealth. Rather than reducing the negative effects of externalities, governments seem to have subsidised them with public funds. Similarly, instead of supplying goods and services that the private sector fail to, governments have, through their expenditure, ensured the minimum number of these goods under the façade of austerity. Furthermore, rather than transferring wealth to the lower class so as to redistribute wealth and reduce inequality, fiscal authorities seem to have done the very opposite.

Evidently, capitalist fiscal policy has many flaws that require scrutiny. It is therefore crucial that we investigate this subject further, so as to gain a more comprehensive understanding of it. This chapter shall henceforth be split into two sections; taxation and government expenditure, after which Islamic fiscal policy will be presented as an effective alternative.

<u>DIRECT AND INDIRECT TAXATION:</u>

Taxation is putatively a tool to equalise income/wealth, reduce negative externalities and raise funds for public expenditure. There are generally two types of tax; the first is direct, on matters such as income/wealth, whilst the second is indirect, in the form of GST (goods and services tax), VAT (value added tax), et cetera. Since the late 18th century, income tax has remained a de-facto form of direct taxation whilst indirect taxation has varied in many forms. Most economies implement a progressive scheme in which direct tax rates rise with income.

Although this may seem fair and equitable, in most respects, capitalist based taxation seems to be an ineffective method of achieving the aforementioned objectives. It is well understood that income based taxation is systemically partial; in that men who are rich in capital but do not work are not taxed, whilst those who earn the same but depend on their income differently are taxed equally. This inequity has kindled inequality such that the rich are able to walk free with their capital whilst the poor are crushed by heavy tax burdens.

Furthermore, tax systems under capitalism maintain a common theme of obscurity. As a result, there are many loopholes that the elite often exploit to minimise costs; wether that be through evading or avoiding taxation. The fact that such malpractice is just within legality is certainly telling of capitalism's inability to tackle corruption. Further still, lower tax revenues (due to rampant exploitation) have actually led to higher tax rates upon those with neither the knowledge nor the ability to avoid paying them - less from elite must be met by more from dregs; loose tax structures have therefore led to harsh inequality.

In this regard, income based taxation is an ostensible method to equalise society, as the poor and destitute face a higher incidence than the rich and powerful. Even when they benefit monetarily, the upper echelon are still known to offshore their earnings to tax havens like Switzerland or Luxembourg, so as to minimise the rate at which their wealth erodes.

The source of such corruption is a system that allows it and a mentality which promotes it. As for the former, capitalism favours the wealthy over the poor and it consequently permits the rich to exploit loopholes whilst punishing the destitute for failing to pay. As for the latter, the concept of cost minimisation by all means necessary has naturally persuaded those who are able (insofar as they are rich, wealthy and acquainted) to avoid direct taxation by either legislatively exploiting the system or simply by offshoring their capital. This is perhaps epitomised by the 2016 Panama papers leaked from Mossack Fonseca; approximately 11.5 million records essentially highlighted the way in which many high level profiles had been offshoring vast sums of wealth through banks and shadow companies.[77]

As for indirect taxes, these are levied by the government and collected by an intermediary. They can branch off into many types such as value added tax, tariffs, sales tax, goods and services tax, et cetera. However, as it stands, many in society are becoming increasingly frustrated with these taxes, due to their exorbitance and multitudinousness. Disgruntled agents have subsequently resulted in deconstructive decisions. With a higher tax incidence, households and corporations have become more conservative, such that for the former, the propensity to save has risen beyond the propensity to spend, and for the latter, production, wages and employment have fallen due to higher markups. This has been detrimental to the economy as it has engendered lower consumption and anaemic growth.

The combination of both direct and indirect tax, amounts to almost half an individuals real earnings, forcing them to survive on little, enjoy fewer luxuries and in an increasingly common case, people are unable to afford basic necessities even whilst working. As a result, many have lost the incentive to enter the labour market and have turned to the governments support, forming a permanent underclass and a welfare state, which has raised both government transfers and the unemployment rate. Evidently, the current tax system has many structural flaws that are becoming increasingly problematic to manage, which has severely damaged the states ability to revitalise the economy.

Bowler, 2015 [77]

GOVERNMENT EXPENDITURE:

Hitherto, we have focused primarily on how much governments spend as opposed to where they spend it. Through the latter lens, one would come to realise that throughout capitalism's existence, governments have focused much of their wealth on patching up the economy from symptoms of a deeper issue. As a result, money is often spent in wasteful means (in that there is a large opportunity cost), rather than productively (which can only be done once the root cause is addressed).

For example, since the financial crisis of 2008 the UK has spent roughly £1.162 trillion (mostly from taxpayer funds) in an attempt to revive the economy from decline.[78] This vast amount of money has been used to crack down on tax evasion, pay off public debt, bail out banks, recuperate toxic assets, manage unemployment and mend many other systemic problems faced by the capitalist economic system. One must realise that had the crisis (and by extension the cyclical phenomena associated with the free market) been averted in the first instance, government expenditure could have been used much more productively elsewhere.

However, some may argue that such faith is slightly naïve, given that governments have consistently been exposed for their corruption in managing public funds. For example, in 2009, the Telegraph released a chilling report detailing the expenses of UK parliament members, each of whom had grossly misused the people's wealth for personal interests and gain on matters such as housing, sustenance, travel, et cetera. In fact, this sort of corruption was epitomised when Western governments used trillions of taxpayer funds, to sustain chaotic wars in both Afghanistan and Iraq, upon a pretext that the world later found to be utterly erroneous.

It is certainly clear from the aforementioned that fiscal policy has become an ephemeral means to correct a chronic illness and a tool to satisfy both political and economic self-interests as opposed to helping the economy function more efficiently.

---

[78] Bukhari, ND

ISLAMIC FISCAL POLICY:

The main objective of fiscal policy in Islam is clear; it is a mechanism for raising and distributing wealth, not a means to hoard and abuse it. This is achieved primarily by taxing surplus wealth as opposed to income. Under the Islamic economic system, there are no progressive and or regressive tax structures per se, rather tax is levied upon set percentages of wealth. In fact, the necessity for wealth based taxation is a matter that is stressed even by notable economists such as Thomas Piketty, who even suggested progressive wealth based taxation in order to equalise capital and level inequality.[79]

Indeed, the underlying purpose behind such a scheme in Islam is to raise the obligatory funds for expenditure and to transfer wealth from the rich to the poor so that a stable middle class is predominant and wealth is collectively enjoyed amongst every individual in society. Let us take a look at how problems under the current system are resolved under Islamic fiscal policy.

I.   **High tax incidence:** Islam forbids any form of indirect taxation (such as VAT and GST). They are considered to be a repressive burden that reduce living standards due to lower purchasing power. Imposing taxes outside of what the *sharia* has defined is therefore not permitted. Muhammad (ﷺ) said in respect to this: "*He who imposes custom duty would not enter paradise.*"[80] Taxation is levied only on the one who can pay it, this assessment is based on an individual's ability to afford basic necessities and luxuries that ensure a normal living standard. As tax is levied on annual surplus wealth, Islam gives a worker the opportunity to use his income on basic necessities and luxury goods. No taxation is levied on the one who has no surplus wealth (which is a strong motivator for consumer spending and investment). Lower burdens also stimulate spending (due to less conservative households) and can even reduce tax avoidance as households have more disposable income after paying what is due from them.

Piketty, 2013 [79]
Hakim, ND [80]

II. **Weak tax structure:** A weakly enforced tax system is perhaps the most important problem in developed capitalist economies. In addition to this, theories on rational choice and utility maximisation explain why agents are constantly looking to exploit tax loopholes without considering the impact on society. As a result of deregulation, agents have incurred high tax deficits, which have had major ramifications on government budget and debt levels. Unlike capitalism, Islam does not differentiate between tax avoidance and tax evasion, rather the *sharia* is strict when agents (who have been appraised to be in a position to pay) do not allow the state to tax their surplus wealth. Such exploitation is a grave matter and the state is obliged to account the one who refuses to pay what is due of him.

III. **Poor expenditure policies:** As we have seen, a lot of a budget is often used by governments to fix the economy as opposed to strengthening it. Islam eliminates the business cycle and in doing so, prevents the costs incurred from issues such as cyclical unemployment, bailouts, et cetera. As we have seen, poor regulation under the capitalist economy has granted autonomy to powerful agents such as politicians and bankers, to misuse the wealth of the economy. Islam holds the Caliph accountable for his role as an economic authority and establishes a criteria for where the funds of the state are to be allocated. Unlike capitalism, Islam places no mortal above the law. Thus expenditure scandals are treated as a matter of corruption and those involved are removed or accounted accordingly.

The Islamic economic system implements a range of set taxes, such as the '*zakah*', which is a low re-distributive tax of 2.5% that is relatively harsher on the rich due to their surplus wealth. Revenues made from this tax are handed to the destitute who cannot afford basic necessities, the needy who live on very little and even the debtors, who are struggling with their arrears. In addition to this, Islam also levies the '*kharaj*' and '*ushr*', which are essentially land based taxes that vary according to area and potential. Under Islam, the state has the authority to confiscate privately owned land after a certain period of time (3 years), providing it is not being used to dissect its evaluated potential benefit. This land is then given to those who will make use of it and produce that benefit to society. Common examples of this occur in less developed countries but it is also apparent in the Western world where private corporations and rich individuals often purchase large plots of land that have the potential to bring many fruits to the economy but remain untouched and idle. Islam also levies other forms of taxation such as a public property tax and the '*jizya*', which is meant for non-muslims who can afford it, providing they meet a specific criteria (male, mature, et cetera). Furthermore, this tax is not fixed like the *zakat,* and so it is not a means to oppress the non-believers, in fact, contrary to popular belief, history has shown that it was frequently lower than what most believers had to pay.

In response to these taxes that are neither exorbitant nor innumerable, economists are often tentative as to whether or not Islamic taxation is sufficient to sustain government expenditure. However, this judgment is relative and often based on current expenditure levels that are required to sustain and expand the economy. As we have clearly seen, there are many cyclical costs that government face under capitalism, which have deceptively raised the bar for expenditure. This, coupled with an incessant growth based mentality has pushed spending to levels that are clearly beyond a states capacity, purely for rapid, short term expansion. By removing cyclical issues and redefining the economic imperative, Islam is able to funnel large sums of money back into the state's budget, allowing governments to spend less on bailing out banks (as an example) and more on improving the welfare of society.

It is important to note that the corruption of those in power under the current capitalist system often go unnoticed. Citizens under an Islamic economy would feel comforted knowing that playing with the money of the people is considered a severe crime under Islam, whether it be a private corporation or even the Caliph himself; no one is above the law and criminals are accounted accordingly under the Islamic judicial system.

On this matter, the Messenger of Allah (ﷺ) is reported to have said: "*He who takes money from the people with the intention of repaying it, Allah will repay it on his behalf, and he who takes it with the intention to waste it, Allah will waste him.*"[81]

As for the allocation of public money, the Islamic economic system is composed of a fixed set of permanent expenditure policies where the state's budget is directed. Some of the main permanent revenues are the *Zakat, I'aalah* that is used for financial support, *Badal* that is used for public allowance, *Maslaha* that is used for public welfare, *Irfaq* that is used for public utilities and emergency funds that are at a time of crisis. Each form of expenditure is designed to manage the health of the economy by ensuring basic necessities and better standards of living are met for each citizen, in all respects.

BAIT UL-MAL:

To manage a budget, Islam would inaugurate the '*Bait ul-Mal*' (treasury fund or quite literally 'the house of funds'). This is an entity that acts as a source for expenditure and recipient for revenue. In other words, it is a permanent, multipurpose fiscal budget that is used as a resource allocation and accounting mechanism for the entire economy. Tax revenues from the *kharaj/ushr*, *jizya*, *zakah*, et cetera, all enter the *Bait ul-Mal*. Expenditures exit in the form of financial support, income for those at service to the state, public welfare, public utilities and other matters related to the state's spending.

The main benefit of such an entity is its dedicated function to organise an economy's funds so as to prevent large debts and budget deficits. In addition to this, the treasury fund is relatively transparent compared to the opaque fiscal institutions under capitalism, whose decisions require third-party analysis for public exposition. One of the core issues with a capitalist budget is that it is often settled (in both expenditure and taxation) for a term. The economy is then geared to work towards fulfilling a specific target in the short run with little consideration for the economy's dynamism.

---

[81] Al-Bukhari, ND

In Islam, the areas for government expenditure are permanent and are derived from the *sharia*, much like the sources of tax revenue. This alleviates a lot of pressure off the Caliph and his assistants as there is unanimity over where the funds of the state must be spent. With better economic clarity agents are also able to plan in the long run according to what the *sharia* has stipulated. This is antithetical to the poorly organised capitalist budget that changes often, depending on the one who manages it and the volatile/unpredictable economic climate.

So the objective of the *Bait ul-Mal* is to collect what is due from the people, whilst they (the people) are aware of what should be taken from them. It is also to spend on the people according to what the *sharia* has stipulated, whilst they are aware of what areas the state must spend on. This does not mean that the Caliph has no control over government spending, rather that there are obligations he must fulfil. As for the areas where he himself apportions public wealth in respect to the *sharia* and the sectors it has defined, this (and the amount) should be explicit to the people, such is their right under Islam.

One could also argue that the *Bait ul-Mal* behaves like a fiscal union, in that it unifies fiscal policy for the whole state according to what the *sharia* has stipulated and is the central source for tax revenues and expenditure. Indeed, this is truly beneficial for the Islamic government as it prevents individual provinces from developing different fiscal policies even if they are under the perimeter of the *sharia*. This would cause disorder, resulting in misdirected expenditure and taxation, ultimately damaging the state's budget.

Finally, if we look to the prodigious history of Islam and its implementation, we find that the Islamic economy was rich in public wealth, such that the Caliphate did not know what to use it for. This was a common occurrence under the Abbasid, Mameluke, Umayyad and Ottoman era. Such wealth could have only been accumulated through an efficient fiscal structure (*Bait ul-Mal*) that effectively managed the funds of the state, in line with Islamic fiscal policy.

XII. UNEMPLOYMENT

Synopsis: *Systemic issues coupled with ineffective economic policy, are two core reasons why unemployment still pervades developed capitalist economies.*

Unemployment is yet another epidemic issue within the free market system. Although ubiquitous, empirical data shows that the number of unemployed (globally) has gradually contracted since the financial crisis. Whilst it is certainly true that unemployment is at its lowest, this should not detract from the real problem; that roughly 1.69 million people in the UK alone are currently without work.[82a] Lest this diminishing figure deceive us, it is worth noting that unemployment peaked in 2011 at 2.68 million due to the harsh effects of the sub-prime mortgage crisis and that at any given time between 2000 to 2015, approximately 1.5 to 2.5 million people have consistently been unemployed within the United Kingdom.[82b]

The consequences of unemployment are well understood in contemporary economy theory. Persistently high levels create severe long term social costs such as a loss of income and a reduction in one's quality of life (living standards). This can also reduce spending power, leading to more conservative households and even anaemic aggregate demand. A diminishing labour market also contracts an economy's long run aggregate supply, creating a large opportunity cost to gross domestic product. In fact, economists use the term 'hysteresis' to describe the situation in which a negative output gap (due to high unemployment and spare capacity), leads to deflationary pressure (and by extension a reduction in profits and output).

There are also fiscal costs associated with unemployment; a fall in tax revenues and higher government expenditure on welfare payments (transfers) has forced larger budget deficits and greater levels of public debt. Furthermore, perhaps the greatest problem with a contracting labour market due to unemployment is social deprivation and growing levels of inequality, which is particularly evident in developed capitalist economies.

---

[82] ONS, 2014

This chapter shall focus primarily on structural unemployment within the capitalist labour market. That being said, it is worth defining the other forms of unemployment so as to understand the various policies enacted to combat them. Unemployment can therefore be categorised into the following:

I. **Frictional unemployment:** When workers lose their jobs but are also in the process of looking for new work. That is to say they are merely transitioning between jobs.

II. **Cyclical unemployment:** When workers lose their jobs due to a downturn in aggregate demand. A phenomenon which is inherent within the business cycle.

III. **Structural unemployment:** When workers lose their jobs due to an imbalance between the demand and supply of skills. That is to say unemployment is caused by structural issues and inefficiencies within the labour market.

IV. **Seasonal unemployment:** When workers lose their jobs due to a change in the demand for labour, which fluctuates at the behest of seasons during the year.

V. **Real-wage unemployment:** When workers lose their jobs due to an imbalance between the demand and supply of labour, which is common during a recession, when firms seek to cut labour surplus as opposed to lowering wages.

To note, unemployment is also contingent on the economies climate. In other words, high levels of unemployment often arise during a recession/contraction, whilst lower levels are present during a recovery/expansion.

Capitalism's existence is tainted with crises, leading to regular fluctuations in the rate of unemployment. Hitherto, this book has shown how Islam provides an alternative to such volatility but this is not to say that unemployment would be non-existent under an Islamic economy. It is therefore important to compare policies that are currently in use to rectify the problem.

CAUSES AND IMMEDIATE REMEDIES:

Structural unemployment stems from three main sources; minimum wage legislation, labour market regulation and unionisation. Each have a commonality in that they are an interference with the markets capacity to allocate labour. Higher minimum wages, stricter labour market regulation and a greater degree of unionisation all lead to more pressure on wages, which raise costs for firms and businesses, shifting the wage setting curve to the right, causing the natural rate of unemployment to increase (see appendix XII).

The rapid growth in trade unions (particularly in the mid 20th century) coupled with incessant government intervention (particularly post Keynesianism) has led to a poor labour market, often characterised by high and volatile levels of unemployment. However, the Islamic economic system has an impressive set of policies that completely suppress each of these sources, immediately providing stability to the level of employment and the overall labour market.

In regards to minimum wage and labour market regulations, Islam prohibits price controls entirely and as a result tampering with the wage level is not permissible. To remain competitive, firms would have to set wages according to the market instead of being forced by government intervention. As such, the market is able to decided the level of employment in accordance with the demand and supply for labour. Islam also prohibits the formation of trade unions (unionisation). Whilst this may be a shock to some, it is the duty of both parties to agree on a labour contract, so that both sides are content. As such, it is forbidden to strike against the employer after the employee has signed a contract and any violation of this agreement can be dealt with through the state's judges.

Evidently then, Islam eradicates some of the key sources of unemployment by implementing policies that work to prevent exogenous labour market interference, ultimately paving the way for a stable level of employment (see appendix XIII).

CRITICISMS OF CAPITALISM'S POLICY:

I. **Monetary stimulus:** This policy aims to stimulate output (and thus the demand for labour) through expansionary monetary policy (see appendix XIV). This involves reducing interest rates to encourage borrowing, which ultimately provides households with more money for expenditure. Alternatively, the central bank is able to pursue open market operations which also increases aggregate demand, forcing firms and businesses to hire more labour. However, the issue with such a policy, is that it invites inflation in the long run. To fix one problem the economy would be creating another, just as bad. As we saw in chapter five, inflation often leads to a fall in real incomes, and as a result, households reduce consumption due to lower purchasing power, which can result in a higher level of unemployment. The effects of such a policy may seem attractive in the short run but as time passes, it is clear that the negative externalities on the economy merely reverse the action taken to reduce unemployment itself.

II. **Fiscal stimulus:** This policy aims to stimulate aggregate demand (and thus the demand for labour) through expansionary fiscal policy (see appendix XV). This involves cutting consumer taxes or transferring wealth to firms and businesses in order to stimulate employment. The former unlocks more disposable wealth amongst consumers and as a result, firms hire more to meet the demand. Whilst the latter incentivises higher production (providing it is profitable), which raises the level of employment. The issue with lower taxes is a fall in tax revenue, which is likely to induce a higher budget deficit. As for the higher transfers to firms and business, this is often backed by debt, due to the large amount of money required to stimulate aggregate demand. Fiscal stimulus is also counter effective in the long run as stimulus pushes up the interest rate, which crowds out investors. This further reduces aggregate demand and the economy can, at times, be left with the very same issue this policy tried to amend.

III. **Fiscal retrenchment (austerity):** Austerity is essentially the tightening of fiscal policy and it is usually adopted during times of severe economic decline in order to stimulate growth. However, governments regularly use austerity measures to try and reduce unemployment by restoring investor confidence. The aim is therefore to stimulate investment and aggregate demand, which leads to higher levels of employment (see appendix XVI). This policy has received heavy criticism after governments sustained long-term austerity measures post crisis. For some, it is considered an ineffective method of stimulating employment simply due to the budget cuts it involves. As a result of a lack of spending, economies undergo anaemic growth which could even lead to a climate, worse than the one austerity sought to control. It is also not a permanent fix, the systemic issues within capitalism mean that governments often have to increase their budget deficits in order to deal with cyclical issues, these particular problems also drive investment down and essentially work to counter government austerity measures. Furthermore, retrenchment has led to large uproar within capitalist societies for very obvious reasons, which is a growing concern for policy makers, due to political dissidence and general instability.

IV. **Reducing labour off-shoring:** Off-shoring is essentially when businesses partake in the act of relocating to other low-cost countries to reduce their costs. To combat this phenomenon, 're-shoring' (where companies are given incentives to return) is supposedly an effective method to raise domestic employment. However, the disadvantage of such a policy can be appreciated on a wider, more international scale, where the problem of unemployment merely shifts geographically. This is an issue when considering areas like the eurozone, as companies that shift internally between countries would essentially mean that unemployment has moved from one part to another, but it has not been resolved. It is clear that anti-labour off-shoring policies are merely a temporary fix (an ineffective one at that) to a more chronic problem.

V. **Improving education and work experience:** Although this may seem effective at reducing unemployment (higher education and experience is akin to a stronger work force), it would have a limited impact on the deeper and more critical issues under the free-market. Increasing the opportunities for education would not be as fruitful due to the current high demand for experience. As a result of this selective approach by firms and businesses, many youth remain unemployed and are often undervalued. The issue here is that there currently exists a surplus of labour but a mismatch in opportunity. A growing population would only mean more frictional unemployment. In other words, such a policy improves the quality of the labour force but fails to get them hired. This is not to say it isn't effective, rather not suited for the system problem capitalism suffers from.

These are some of the core market policies used to combat unemployment. The criticisms in this chapter illustrate capitalism's cyclical problem, in that to solve a problem policymakers must give rise to yet another. Let us turn our attention to the Islamic economic system in the hope of locating a more permanent answer to the issue of unemployment.

ISLAM'S ANSWER TO UNEMPLOYMENT[83]:

I. **Maintaining a strong SME sector:** Policies that seek to maintain competition within the market are often effective in curing unemployment. Monopolies in a capitalist economy tend to supply less and cut costs more, as a result, they are generally considered poor job creators. In Islam, regulated markets eradicate highly imperfect competition and level the market, thus making companies more effective in hiring workers by providing opportunities to the labour force. A small-medium based enterprise market collectively act as a better alternative to large firms that control the market as supply is not deliberately cut back and the labour force is not reduced as the factors of production are not all concentrated in the hands of one firm with profit maximising intentions.

II. **Eliminating cyclical unemployment:** An end to the business cycle would mean a drastic reduction in long term issues within the labour market, especially in terms of unemployment. Economic downturns lead to reduced aggregate demand and as a result of labour surplus, firms often cut back on workers. The eradication of such volatility would lead to a more stable economy that does not suffer from large busts and booms, which ultimately means a more stable and permanent rate of employment.

III. **Increasing financial investment:** Financial investment is an effective way of stimulating employment; the greater the investment, the more wealth firms and business can use to pay a larger number of workers, opening new avenues in the labour market. Due to volatile prices and fluctuating interest rates, investors do not rise to their potential under capitalism. In Islam, stable prices and a lack of interest, would attract a higher level of financial investment. A more stable economy would also improve investment due to higher investor confidence in the economy's progression and better economic planning. As a result of a more investor friendly environment, firms and business have more funds to begin hiring more workers.

IV. **Effectively distributing wealth:** A better distribution of wealth would mean economies are less dependant on funds gained from the labour market. This is a concept discussed by many economists and Islam provides an effective mechanism of producing such an effect. In capitalism, the labour market is a key source for sustenance and so unemployment can severely impact the economy, whereas under the Islamic economic system, unemployment would not be so harsh due to better wealth distribution.

V. **Avoiding the poverty trap:** It is well known that under the capitalist system, benefits can be a disincentive for people to enter the labour market. In some cases it can also be more economical for some to remain jobless than to work and receive a lower and or equivalent income. The Islamic economic system would ensure that the basic necessities of man are satisfied whilst primarily obliging work upon those who are capable. That being said, it is important to ensure that the system of guaranteeing basic necessities does not overlap the profitability of earning from a job. This would mean that there is a greater desire to exert effort to attain luxury items rather than being content with basic goods and services.

However, many accuse the Islamic economic system of being susceptible to this very issue. The claim being that providing there are jobs, a lack of focus on production and a strong focus on distribution would reduce the motivation to work within the labour market. This is because a more efficient distributive system is akin to guaranteed basic necessities, causing a reduction in activity due to social contentment. In reality this argument is faulty. Islam is not a welfare state and basic necessities are not handed out to the one who is able to work but chooses not to, in an environment where there are jobs available. After it is clear that effort has been made or there are genuine reasons for such stagnancy, only then are provisions granted. If there are no jobs available then the burden falls on the state to deliver these basic goods as the opportunity does not exist.

Additionally, Islamic economic concepts shape the behaviour of man by obliging him to earn, so as to make use of what Allah (ﷻ) has granted him as provisions in this life. Furthermore, man is never content with purely satisfying his basic necessities rather it is in his nature to demand more after the former is secured. The following evidence epitomises Islam's advocation for work, so as to earn the provisions set out by Allah (ﷻ):

"And say: Work; so Allah will see your work and (so will) His Apostle and the faithful; and you shall be brought back to the Knower of the unseen and the seen, then He will inform you of what you did."[84]

Quran, 9:105 [84]

VI. **Diminishing discrimination:** As a consequence of certain tendencies within capitalist based societies, discrimination in the labour market is rampant and often based on superficialities such as ethnicity, race, religion, et cetera. Furthermore, the bar for skills has continuously risen, which has kindled inequality. As a result, society constrains employment to a narrow criteria. Contrastingly, Islam does not differentiate man based on his ethnicity, race, aesthetic, or any other superficiality for that matter. Rather, man is treated as an equal citizen of the state and if he is skilled and capable for a position it is impermissible to discriminate against him over others based on the aforementioned nonsense. Furthermore, a better outlook on phenomenon such as immigration, would mean higher aggregate demand and spending for Islamic economies, which would ultimately raise the demand for labour.

VII. **Improving the labour force:** Whilst it is clear that improving education and work experience is a policy to combat unemployment, we have seen that it is ineffective in solving the root cause of unemployment. It must be noted that this is a problem specific to capitalism. As stated, the issue in a capitalist economy is not that society lacks experience rather it is that they are unable to find a job. Islam opens more avenues than capitalism could ever dream of doing and as a result, it no longer becomes ineffective to improve the labour force through factors such as education, rather it is a means to strengthen it.

XIII. EPILOGUE: PARADIGM SHIFT

This book has covered a wide range of deep rooted issues within the free market; from problems in its foundation to cracks within its framework. As we have seen, the oratory that blinds man from realising the failure of capitalism is but a blindfold wrapped by the capitalists themselves. In darkness and general ignorance, society has grown to accept that there is nothing to illuminate the subject that has been submerged in mathematical and statistical jargon. However, Islam came to simplify what has been made esoteric, to resolve what has been made problematic and succeed that which has miserably failed.

In this book, we journeyed through key problems faced by capitalism, not merely as an economic system but also as an ideology. We noted failures within its principles, an erroneous economic problem, the manifestations of these aforementioned inconsistencies in terms of inequality, market failure, business cycles, financial crises, policy failure, et cetera. In each case, we found that capitalism failed to solve the very problems it created and that the Islamic system consistently brought forth a viable alternative; contending the current narrative and more importantly, solving the contemporary issues faced by mankind.

If the paradigm highlighted in this book continues to persist, let there be no doubt; the free market will edge towards its last breath and whilst capitalism tinkers on the brink of collapse, men will ponder over what could possibly replace it. To them we must say; Islam is the rich and intelligible ideology that will be the first to replace bankrupt capitalism.

Muslims will find solace in knowing that we are on the verge of radical change and that the time ahead of us will be far more important than the history we once left behind. Islam will not only dominate the economic sphere, it will excel in every aspect of life and it shall rip the blindfold held by the hand of the capitalist around the eyes of man, enlightening him to the truth, that is the beauty and vigour of the Islamic ideology.

This book will therefore end on an apt verse from the Holy Quran, where Allah (ﷻ) says: "...*This day, I have perfected your religion for you, completed My Favour upon you, and have chosen for you Islam as your religion...*"[85]

XIV. BIBLIOGRAPHY

BOOKS AND JOURNALS:

- Al-Bukhari, M. (ND 810 -870). *Ṣaḥīḥ al-Bukhārī*. Muhammad al-Bukhari.

- Alkhateeb, F. (2014). *Lost Islamic History.* C Hurst & Co (Publishers) Ltd.

- Al-Nasā'ī, A. (ND 829 -915). *As-Sinan al-Kubra*. Abd ar-Raḥmān al-Nasā'ī.

- An-Nabhani, T. (1990). *The Economic System of Islam.* Al-Khilafah Publications.

- At-Tirmidhi, M. (270 Dhu-al-Hijjah). *Jāmi' At-Tirmidhi*. Muhammad at-Tirmidhi.

- Bojicic, S. (2010). *America ... America ... Or Is It?* AuthorHouse. Pg 243.

- Ford, H. (1922). *My Life and Work*. Garden City.

- Friedman, M. (1987). *Quantity Theory of Money*. Palgrave Macmillan.

- Ibn al-Hajjaj, M. (ND 821-875). *Ṣaḥīḥ Muslim.* Muslim ibn al-Hajjaj.

- Ibn Hanbal, A. (ND 780 -855). *Musnad Ahmad ibn Hanbal*. Aḥmad ibn Ḥanbal.

- Jevons, William S. (1871). *The Theory of Political Economy*. Macmillan & Co.

- Keynes, John M. (1936). *The General Theory of Employment, Interest and Money*. Macmillan.

- Keynes, John M. (1933). *National Self-Sufficiency.* Macmillan. Section 3.

- Mankiw, G and Taylor, P. (2014). *Economics*. 3rd ed. Thomson Learning.

- Marx, K and McLellan, D. (1939). *Grundrisse*. Penguin Classics.

- McCulley, P. (2009). *Global Central Bank Focus.*

- Minsky, Hyman P. (1992). *The Financial Instability Hypothesis*. The Levy Economics Institute.

- Mises, L. (1912). *The Theory of Money and Credit.* J.C.

- Mises, L. (1949). *Human Action: A Treatise on Economics*. Yale University.

- Panarella, A. (1995). *The Maastricht Treaty and the Economic and Monetary Union.*

- Pareto, V. (1906). *Manuale di economia politica.* Società Editrice Libraria.

- Piketty, T. (2013). *Capital in the Twenty First Century.* Belknap Press.

- Praussello, F. (2012). *The Eurozone Experience.* FrancoAngeli.

- Richard, P. (1976). *Antitrust Law: An Economic Perspective.* University of Chicago Press.

- Rochon, L and Rossi, S. (2015). *The Encyclopaedia of Central Banking.* Edward Elgar Pb.

- Roxburgh, Lund and Piotrowsk. (2011). *Mapping global capital markets.* McKinsey Global Institute.

- Samuelson, Paul A. (1947). *Foundations of Economic Analysis.* Harvard University.

- Smith, A. (1776). *The Wealth of Nations.* Emereo Publishing.

- Szostak, R. (1995). *Tech Innovation and the Great Depression.* Westview Press Inc.

- Thornton, P. (2015). *Econom ics Demystified.* Pearson. 1st ed.

- Quran (Translated Meaning of the Quran). Sahih Int. Available: www.quran.com

PAPERS AND ARTICLES:

- Atkinson, Luttrell and Rosenblum. (2013). *Assessing the Costs and Consequences of the 2007 Financial Crisis and its Aftermath. Economic Letter.* 8 (7) Last accessed: 06.04.15.

- BoE. (ND). *A brief history of banknotes.* Available: http://www.bankofengland.co.uk/banknotes/pages/abouthistory.aspx. Last accessed: 05.04.15.

- Bowler, T. (2015). *Global views on the HSBC tax scandal.* Available: http://www.bbc.co.uk/news business-31300712. Last accessed: 01.04.15.

- Buffet, W. (2002). *Berkshire Hathaway Report.* Available: http://www.fintools.com/docs /Warren%20Buffet%20on %20Derivatives.pdf. Last accessed: 05.04.15.

- CR. (2013). *Germany's hyper inflation-phobia.* Available: http://www.economist.com/blogs/freeexchange/2013/11 /economic-history-1. Last accessed: 04.04.15.

- Carter, B. (2014). *Which country has the highest tax rate?* Available: http://www.bbc.co.uk/news/magazine-263 27114. Last accessed: 03.04.15.

- Claire, A. (2012). *It Could Be Worse*. Available: http://blog. redington.co.uk/Articles/And rew-Clare/April-2012/IT-CO ULD-BE-WORSE.aspx. Last accessed: 04.04.15.

- Credit Suisse. (2014). *Global Wealth Report 2014*. Available :https://publications.creditsu isse.com/tasks/render/file/? fileID=60931FDE-A2D2-F5 68-B041B58C5EA591A4. Last accessed 04.04.15.

- Geoghegan, B. (2008). *Remember the last recession?* Available: http://news.bbc.co. uk/1/hi/magazine/7686531.st m. Last accessed: 05.04.15.

- Greenspan, A. (2013). *Never Saw It Coming - Nov/Dec V. 92 No. 6*. Available: https:// www.foreignaffairs.com/arti cles/united-states2013-10-15 /never-saw-it-coming. Last accessed: 05.04.15.

- Gruić, B and Schrimpf, A. (2014). *Highlights of the BIS international statistics*. Available: http://www.bis.org /publ/qtrpdf/r_qt1403b.htm. Last accessed: 04.04.15.

- Hall, M. (2008). *The sub-prime crisis, the credit squeeze and northern rock: The Lessons To Be Learnt*. Journal of Financial Regulation and Compliance. Last accessed: 06.04.15.

- Keen, S. (2014). *Modelling Financial Instability*. Available: http://www.debtdeflation.com/ blogs/2014/02/02/modeling-financial-instability/. Last accessed: 01.04.15.

- Kingsley, P. (2012). *Financial crisis: timeline*. Available: http:// www.theguardian.com/business/ 2012/aug/07/credit-crunch-boom-bust-timeline. Last accessed 05.04.15.

- Knight, L. (2010). *What do investment banks do?* Available: http://www.bbc.co.uk/news business -11211776. Last accessed 03.04.15.

- Macrotrends. (2015). *Gold and Silver Prices - 100 Year Historical Chart*. Available: http://www.macrotrends.net/ 1333/gold-and-silver prices-100-year-historical-chart. Last accessed: 07.04.15.

- Madeleine, P and Stacey, T. (2014). *Unfair and Unclear*. Available: http://www.equality trust.org.uk/sites/default/files/ attachments/resources/Unfair %20and%20Unclear.pdf. Last accessed: 03.04.15.

- McLeay, Radia and Thomas. (2014). *Money creation in the modern economy*. Available: www.bankofengland.co.uk/ publications/Documents/quart erlybulletin/2014qb14q1prere leasemoneycreation.pdf.

- Money, P. (2014). *How to waste £375 billion? (The Failure of Quantitative Easing).* Available: https://www.youtube.com/watch?v=4l06RhFoLE4. Last accessed: 02.04.15.

- NDC. (ND). Available: http://www.nationaldebtclocks.org. Last accessed: 03.04.15.

- NBER. (2010). *US Business Cycle Expansions and Contractions.* Available: http://www.nber.org/cycles.html. Last accessed: 04.04.15.

- Nixon, R. (Video recorded 1971). *Nixon Ends Bretton Woods International Monetary System.* Available: https://www.youtube.com/watch?v=iRzr1QU6K1o. Last accessed: 05.04.15.

- ONS. (2014). *Public Sector Finances, March 2014.* Office for National Statistics. Last accessed: 04.04.15.

- Pettinger, T. (2014). *Money Supply, M0, M3, M4 and Inflation.* Economics Help. http://www.economicshelp.org/blog/5278/inflation/m4-money-supply-and-inflation/ Last accessed: 04.04.15.

- R.A. (2010). *The Volcker recession Who beat inflation?* Available: http://www.economist.com/blogs/freeexchange/2010/03/volcker_recession.

- R.A. (2015). *What is QE?* Available: http://www.economist.com/blogs/economist-explains/2015/03/economist-explains-5. 05.04.15.

- Rickards, J. (2012). *Repeal of Glass-Steagall Caused the Financial Crisis.* Available: http://www.usnews.com//repeal-of-glass-steagall-caused-the-financial-crisis.

- Ro, S. (2014). *The Rise Of The $156 Trillion Market For Global Financial Assets.* Available: http://www.businessinsider.com/156-trillion-global-financial-assets-2014-3?IR=T. Last accessed: 05.04.15.

- Rogers, S. (2011). *Bank reforms :how much did we bail them out and how much do they still owe?* Available: http://www.theguardian com/news/datablog/2011/nov/12/bank-bailouts-uk-credit-crunch. Last accessed: 03.04.15.

- Sandler, L. (2011). *Lehman Borrowed $18 Billion From Previously Secret Fed Program.* Available: http://www.bloomberg.com/news/articles/2011-07-06/lehman-borrowed-18-billion-from-undisclosed-fed-program-during-08-crisis. Last accessed: 05.04.15.

- Snyder, M. (2014). *$1.5 Quadrillion Derivatives Market Collapse In 2015?* Available: http://themillenniumreport.com

/2014/07/will-the-1-5quadrillion-derivatives-market-collapse-in2015. Last accessed: 05.04.15.

- Slaughter and May. (2011). *An Overview of the UK Comp etition Rules.* Available: http://www. slaughter andmay.com/media/1515647/an-overview-of-the-uk-competition-rules.pdf. Last accessed: 05.04.15.

- Syal, R. (2013). *UK's tax gap rises by £1bn to £35bn.* Available: http:/www.theguardian.com/politics/2013/oct/11/uk-tax-gap-rises-hmrc avoidance-nonpayment. Last accessed: 03.04.15.

- NYT. (1937). Financier's Fortune in Oil Amassed in Industrial Era of 'Rugged Individualism'. Available: http://www.standardoiltrust.com. Last accessed 02.04.15.

- Thunder, J. (2014). *Debt Statistics.* Available: http://themoneycharity.org.uk/media/Debt-Stats-Full-May-2014.pdf. Last accessed: 03.04.15.

- Wali, S. (2014). *Breakthrough Economics: Global Unemploy ment and the Islamic Solution.* Available at: http://breakthrou gheconomics.blogspot.co.uk/2014/06/global-unemployment and-islamic-solution.html. Last accessed: 02.04.15.

- Weber, M. (1905). *The Protestant Ethic and Spirit of Capitalism.* Available: https://archive.org/details/protestantethics00webe. Last accessed: 02.04.15.

- Weiner, K. (2014). *Prices Provide a Misleading Measu re of Dollar Devaluation.* http://www.forbes.com/siteskeith weiner/2014/10/13/prices-pro vide-a-misleading-measure-of-dollar-devaluation#3aeb07162 539. Last accessed: 03.04.15.

- World Bank. (2014). *Poverty Overview Report.* Available: http://www.worldbank.org/en/topic/poverty/overview. Last accessed: 02.04.15.

XV. APPENDIX

I. Microeconomic (left) and macroeconomic (right) equilibria between both demand (D/AD) and supply (S/AS/LRAS):

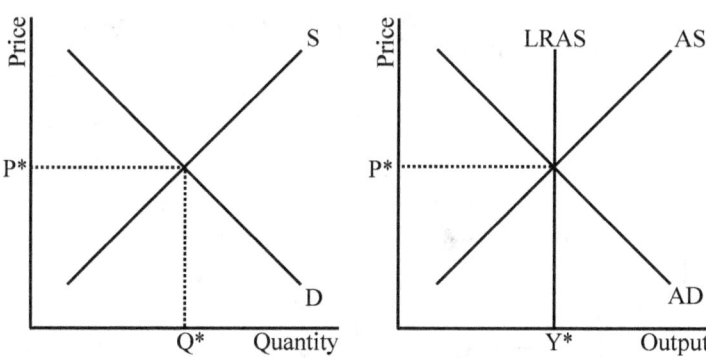

Note: At P*, Q* and Y*, the market/economy is in equilibrium.

II. The Lorenz curve and Gini coefficient/index/ratio:

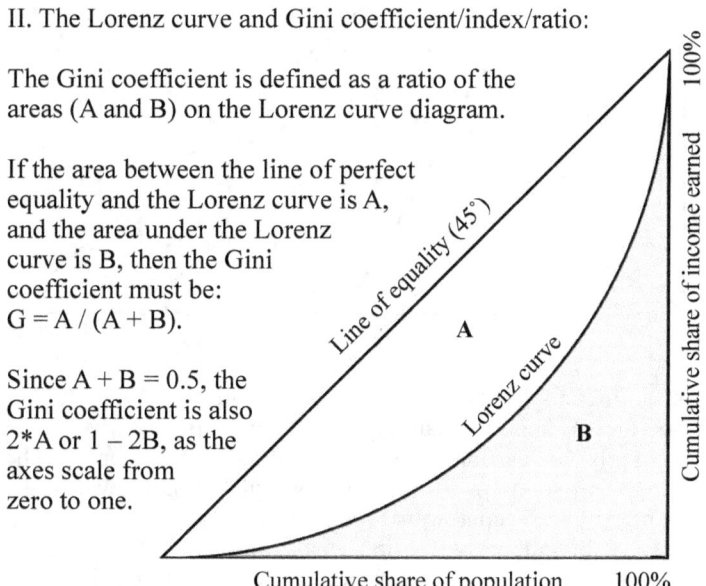

The Gini coefficient is defined as a ratio of the areas (A and B) on the Lorenz curve diagram.

If the area between the line of perfect equality and the Lorenz curve is A, and the area under the Lorenz curve is B, then the Gini coefficient must be: $G = A / (A + B)$.

Since $A + B = 0.5$, the Gini coefficient is also $2*A$ or $1 - 2B$, as the axes scale from zero to one.

III. Highly imperfect competitors (like a monopolist) pose a detrimental threat to the market, particularly in terms of its ability to allocate resources efficiently. The following graph illustrates how a monopoly is able to reduce consumer surplus (specifically by area P_mP_cCA), create deadweight loss (ABC) due to higher pricing (P_c to P_m) and reduce the quantity supplied (Q_c to Q_m) of any given good and or service:

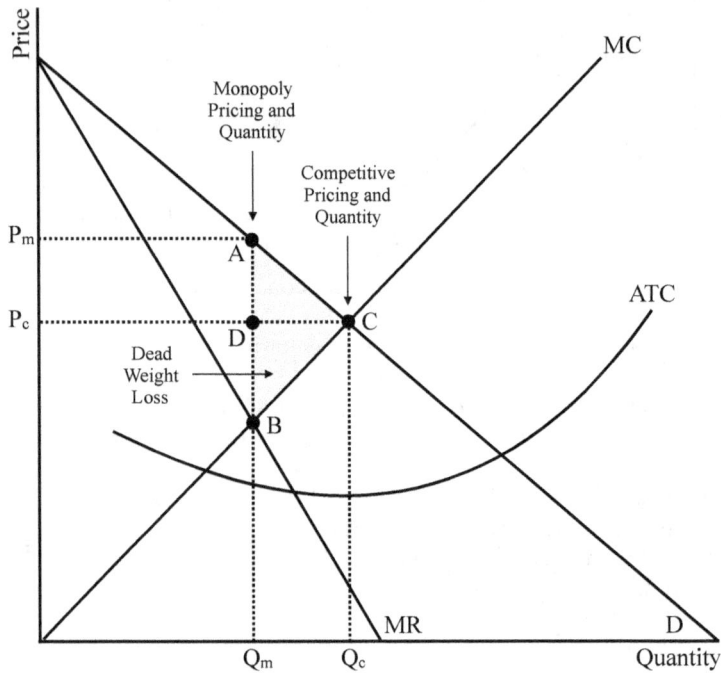

As the monopolised good in question is often inelastic, highly imperfect competition can deprive the economy of what could potentially be a vital resource (in terms of its supply). The deliberate rise in price for this inelastic good, rewards the monopolist with supernormal profit (specifically area P_mP_cDA), whilst simultaneously closing consumption of the good in question to a section of society (often the poor and needy).

IV. Perfectly competitive and monopolistic markets are good approximations. Markets in the Islamic economic system would generally be competitive and although I have yet to realise any models as to what these markets may look like, it may be useful for those who wish to embark on an endeavour of constructing a model, to understand the following market structures.

Below are two graphs; the left is an illustration of equilibrium within a perfectly competitive market, whilst the right is an illustration of equilibrium for an individual firm:

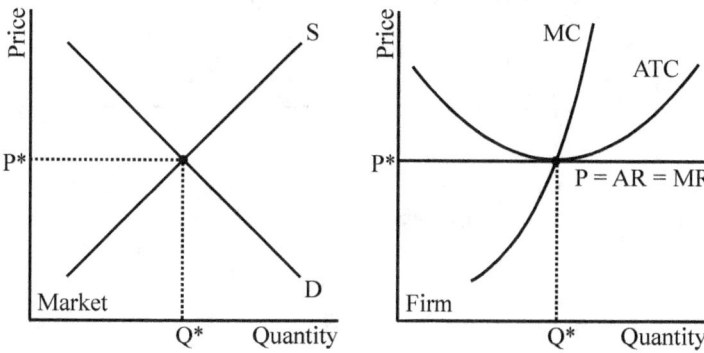

Below are two graphs; the left is an illustration of equilibrium under monopolistic competition in the short run, whilst the right is an illustration of equilibrium in the long run:

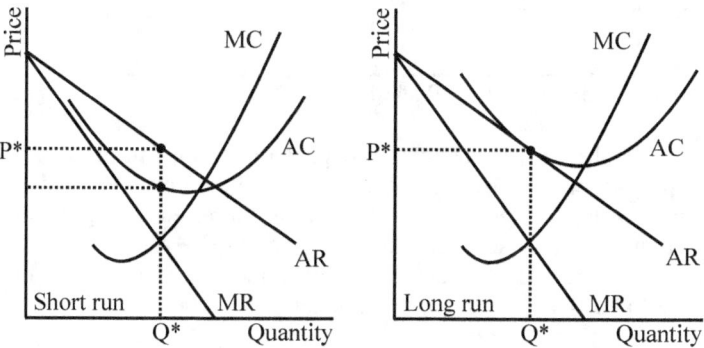

V. Demand-pull inflation (left) caused by a positive shock to aggregate demand and cost-push inflation (right) caused by a negative shock to aggregate supply:

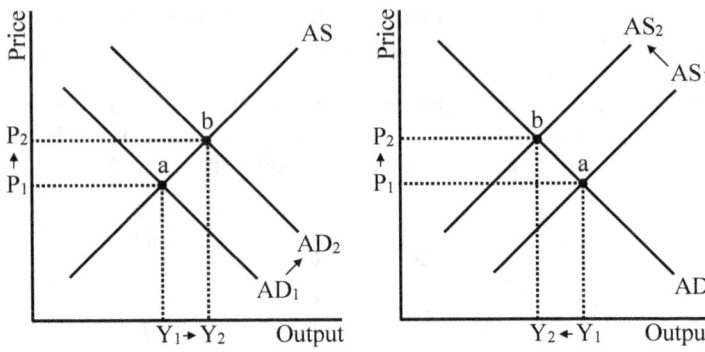

Monetary inflation in the AD-AS model (right) caused by a positive shock to the money supply in the M^s-M^d model (left):

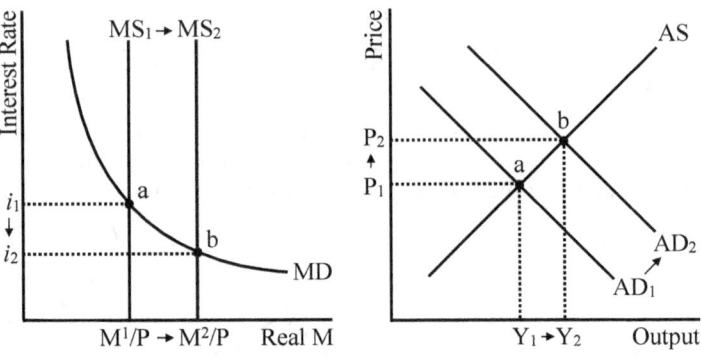

The graphs above illustrate an expansionary shift in the money supply, which causes a reduction in the interest rate and an increase in real money balances. Here, the affect on aggregate demand in a closed economy $[c_0 + c_1(Y-T) + I(Y,i) + G]$ is through investment, whereby a lower interest rate reduces the cost to borrow, shifting aggregate demand to the right.

VI. Demand-pull deflation (left) caused by a negative shock to aggregate demand and cost-push deflation (right) caused by a positive shock to aggregate supply:

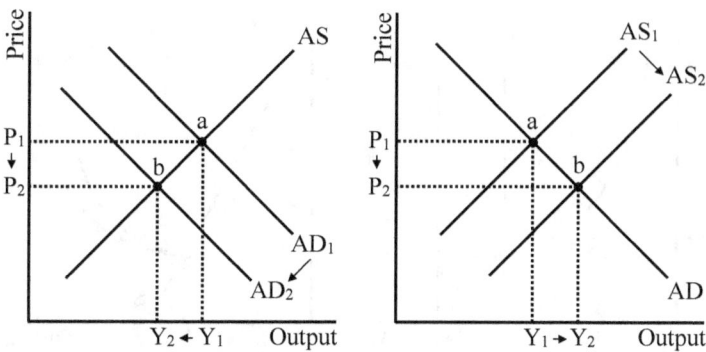

Monetary deflation in the AD-AS model (right) caused by a negative shock to the money supply in the M^s-M^d model (left):

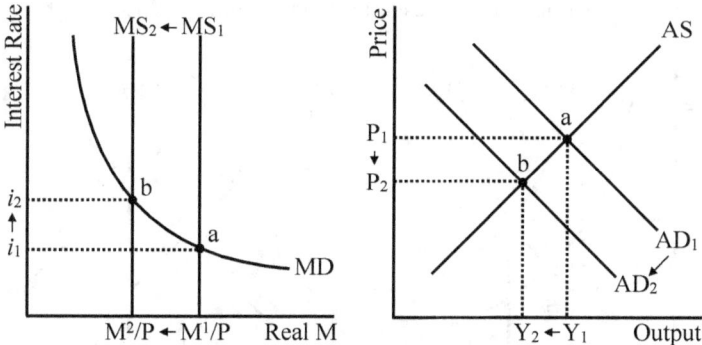

The graphs above illustrate a contractionary shift in the money supply, which causes an increase in the interest rate and a reduction in real money balances. Here, the effect on aggregate demand in a closed economy $[c_0 + c_1(Y-T) + I(Y,i) + G]$ is through investment, where a higher interest rate raises the cost to borrow, shifting aggregate demand to the left.

VII. Liquidity trap; a situation when expansionary monetary policy employed by the central bank becomes ineffective at reducing interest rates (left) and or stimulating output (right):

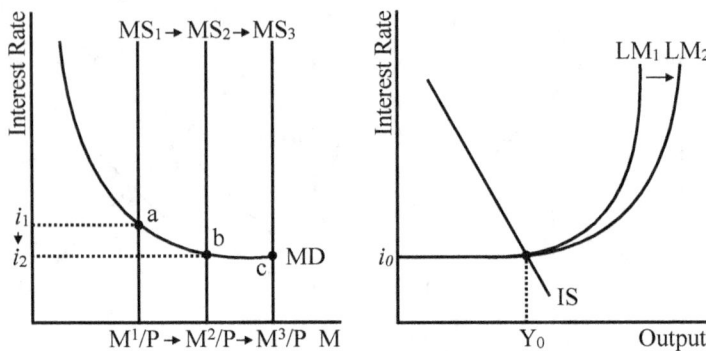

VIII. Fiscal stimulus shifts the IS curve to the right, which increases the interest rate (left) and 'crowds out' investment. Providing the effects of higher spending are greater than that of lower investment, the recessionary gap could be closed (right):

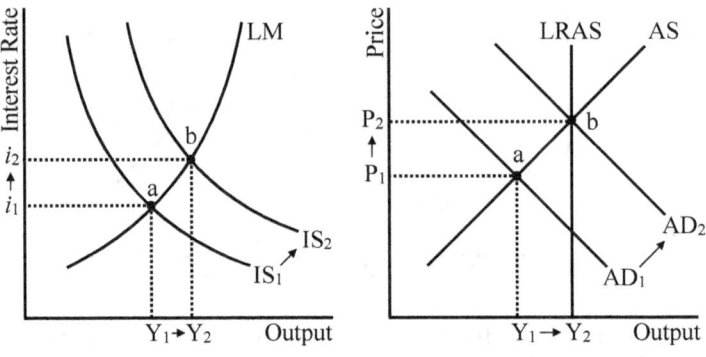

Although fiscal policy raises aggregate demand in the short run, inflation would mean a long run reduction in real money, which pushes the LM curve to the left and output back to its natural rate. Whilst output did not change, its composition did.

IX. Monetary expansion creates inflation in the long run as shown on the IS-LM model (left), which causes aggregate demand to expand as shown on the AD-AS model (right). Due to the neutrality of money, expansionary monetary policy fails to improve growth in the long run and merely results in a higher price level, which shifts LM back to its original position:

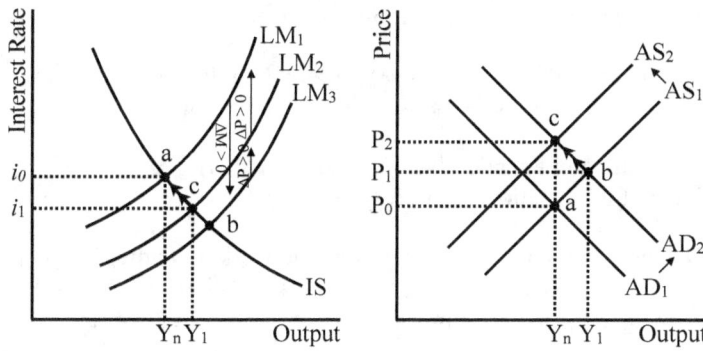

X. The Laffer curve demonstrates the relationship between the tax rate and the amount received in tax revenue. Arthur Laffer himself mentions the origins of such a concept within the writings of Ibn Khaldun, specifically in 'The Muqaddimah':

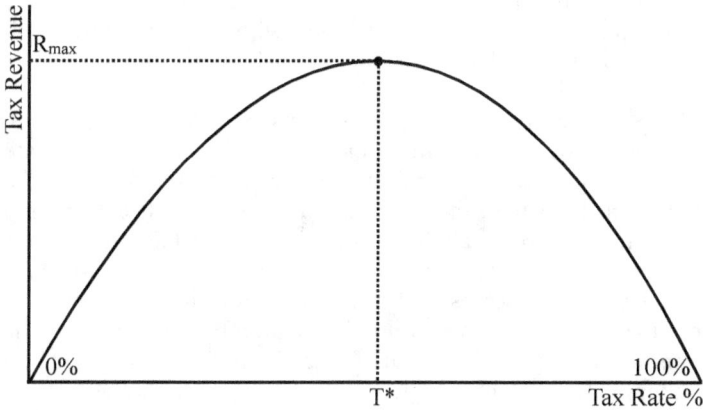

XI. The Solow-Swan growth model is unrestricted by time and excludes both government and trade. Output is produced using two variables; labour (L) and capital (K) in an aggregate production function that satisfies the Inada conditions.

The model is given by: $Y_t = K(t)^\alpha (A(t)L(t))^{1-\alpha}$
The transition equation is given by: $K_{t+1} = K_t(1-d) + sz\sqrt{K_t}$
The output equation is given by: $Y_t = z\sqrt{K_t}$

To find capital and output per worker we divide by N_t
Let $k_t = K_t/N_t$ and $y_t = Y_t/N_t$, N_t is the number of workers

The transition equation becomes: $k_{t+1} = k_t(1-d) + sz\sqrt{k_t}$
The output equation becomes: $y_t = z\sqrt{k_t}$

To find capital and output per effective worker we divide by A_t
Let $k_t^E = K_t/(N_t \cdot A_t)$ and $y_t = Y_t/(N_t \cdot A_t)$, A_t is the productivity growth and N_t is the number of workers. $A_{t+1} = A_t(1+g_A)$

The transition equation becomes:
$k_{t+1}^E = (k_t^E(1-d))/(1+g_A) + (sz\sqrt{k_t^E})/(1+g_A)$
The output equation becomes:
$y_t^E = z\sqrt{k_t^E}$

Growth here is split into two parts. The first is derived from capital accumulation (increases in K), which diminishes in the short run. The second, is concerned with productivity growth (increases in A), which does not diminish in the long run.

The Solow-Swan model also informs us that those who are poor in capital are also more productive, whilst those who are rich are less productive and therefore grind to stagnation in the long run. However, this is a common fate for all as the only variable that can sustain long run growth is productivity.

Higher savings increase the rate at which capital is replenished but merely transfer the level of stagnation to a higher one. The rate of growth is therefore unaffected by higher investment and only affected by technological progress.

XII. Effects on the level of unemployment can be demonstrated using the wage and price setting equations. Higher minimum wages, stricter labour market regulations and unionisation, all lead to a shift in the wage setting curve (left). Alternatively, unemployment can change due to shocks (such as a rise in oil prices) on markups, shifting the price setting curve (right):

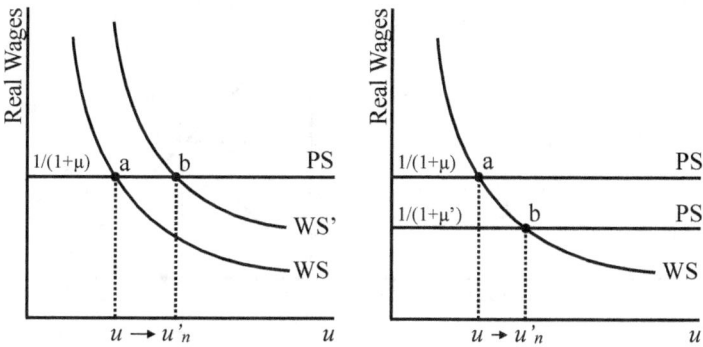

XIII. Unemployment, output and inflation are given by:

Okun's law: $u_t - u_{t-1} = -\beta(g_{yt} - \bar{g}_y)$
Phillips curve: $\pi_t - \pi_{t-1} = -\alpha(u_t - u_n)$
AD relation: $g_{yt} = g_{mt} - \pi_t$

A brief note: Islam maintains an effective response to the Lucas Critique (Lucas, 1976; Sargent, 1987), which essentially states that credibility plays a key role in being able to mitigate inflation via unemployment so as to prevent a contraction.

Unfortunately this credibility has diminished under capitalism and would only return with the establishment of Islam. For under such a system, it is a responsibility on the neck of the ruler to safeguard the Ummah's health.

So long as there is trust in the ruler to obey his Lord, the Caliph can aim for small increases in unemployment to reduce what would be a rare case of inflationary pressure.

XIV. Graphical illustration of a monetary stimulus to reduce unemployment. In the short run, prices and expectations are fixed, so expansionary monetary policy reduces both nominal and real interest rates, leading to higher aggregate demand, more output and consequently higher employment:

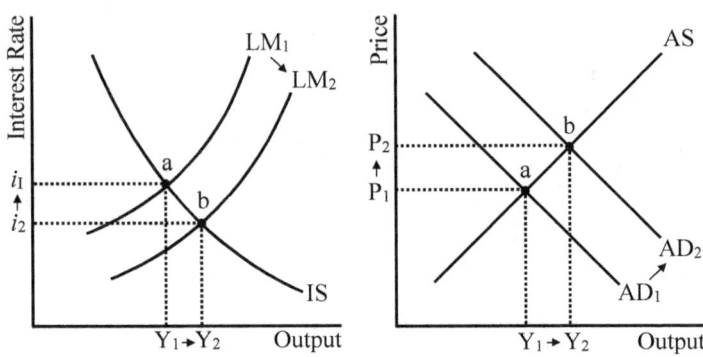

In the long run, increased output and employment raises wages and prices within the labour market. This causes a reduction in the real money supply, an increase in nominal interest rates and, given an expected rise in prices, an increase in real rates:

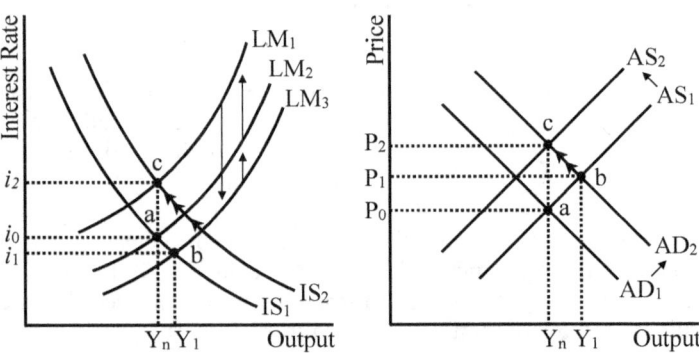

Higher inflation increases price expectations within the market, which leads to an increase in the nominal interest rate above *i*.

XV. Graphical illustration of a fiscal stimulus to reduce unemployment. In the short run, expansionary fiscal policy increases the interest rate, which can deter investment providing savings remain constant. The total impact on output (and thus employment) depends on wether or not the positive effect on Y is greater or less than the negative effect from i:

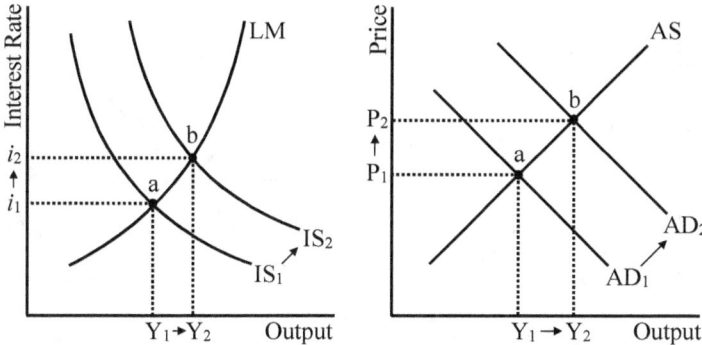

In the long run, output returns to its natural rate through the price mechanism and the labour market with an even higher interest rate. The composition of output merely changes, whereby government spending rises and investment falls:

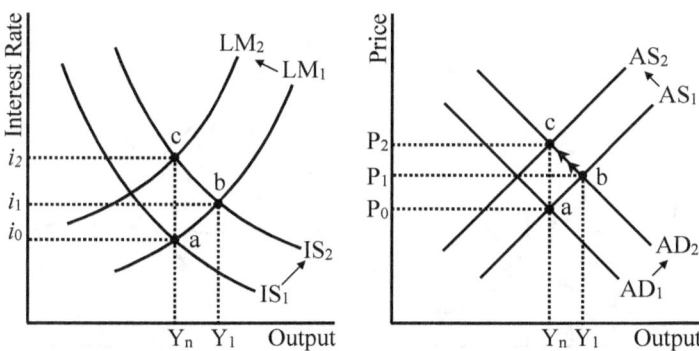

This phenomenon (where higher interest rates from government spending deter investors) is known formally as 'crowding out'.

XVI. Graphical illustration of fiscal retrenchment to reduce unemployment. In the short run, contractionary fiscal policy reduces the interest rate, which can attract investment providing savings remain the same. The total impact on output (and thus employment) depends on wether or not the negative effect on Y is greater or less than the positive effect from i:

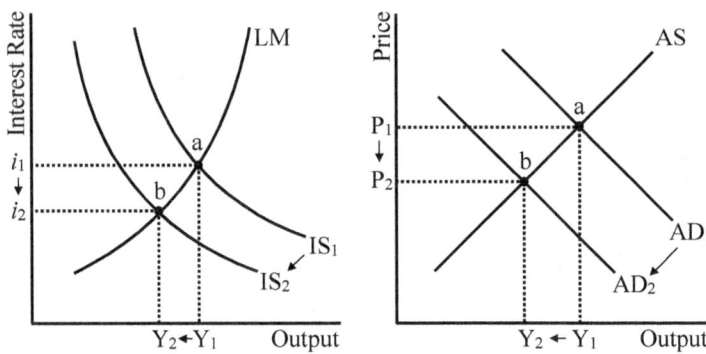

In the long run, output returns to its natural rate through the price mechanism and the labour market with an even lower interest rate. The composition of output merely changes, whereby government spending falls and investment rises:

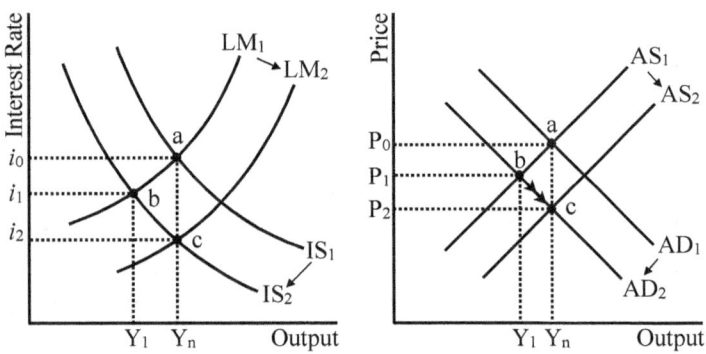

End.